# PICTORIAL HISTORY
## OF THE R.A.F.

PICTORIAL HISTORY OF

# THE R.A.F.

J. W. R. Taylor
and
P. J. R. Moyes

ARCO PUBLISHING COMPANY, Inc.
NEW YORK

# Contents

1974 Printing

Published by ARCO PUBLISHING COMPANY, Inc.
219 Park Avenue South, New York, N.Y. 10003

Library of Congress Catalog Card Number 69–12569
Arco Calalog Number 668–01857–7
Printed in Great Britain

# Introduction

No fighting service has ever had a more appropriate motto than the Royal Air Force. Its parents, the Royal Flying Corps and Royal Naval Air Service, were unwanted babies. Its own birth, on April 1st, 1918, resulted from the forced marriage of those parents, and there were many who regarded the union as an occasion for sorrow rather than joy.

When the R.A.F. was a mere seven months old, the 1914–18 War ended. At once, the older services began to clamour for a return to the former state of affairs in which Britain's air power was divided into two separate components under the direct control of—and completely subservient to—the Army and Navy. Little wonder that those entrusted with the future wellbeing of the young R.A.F. chose for its motto *Per Ardua ad Astra*—Through Difficulties to the Stars.

The difficulties were there from the beginning and were to remain throughout every stage of the life of the Royal Air Force. It was then only a pious hope that the service might one day overcome its difficulties and reach the stars.

This three-volume history, published to mark the 50th birthday of the R.A.F., tells us how well it has borne out the early hopes and of how, paradoxically, in an age when the stars seem almost literally within reach, we are so ungrateful and short-sighted that we are content to let the adult service face a pauper's death. We do so at our own peril, for Britain itself may pass out of existence if this particular life story is allowed to have an unhappy ending.

*January*, 1968.                                                    J.W.R.T.

# Chapter One

# A Stormy Birth

*At my nativity*
*The front of heaven was full of fiery shapes,*
*Of burning cressets; and at my birth*
*The frame and huge foundation of the earth*
*Shak'd like a coward.*

STUDENTS OF SHAKESPEARE will recognise the quotation above as an extract from a speech by Owen Glendower in Act III, Scene I of the First Part of *King Henry IV*. Had Shakespeare lived in our day, he might well have used the same words to describe the birth of the Royal Air Force on April 1st, 1918.

Over in France, the first great air war was filling the heavens daily with fiery shapes, of which all too many were marked with red, white and blue roundels. Far beneath the air battles, the foundation of the earth shak'd indeed as barrage after barrage of artillery fire made tired soldiers cringe closer to the walls of their grave-like trenches.

Nobody at that time doubted the worth of air forces; and when, a generation later, Britain itself became the target for massive air attacks, English housewives willingly sacrificed the precious aluminium pots and pans from their kitchens in the belief that these humble objects could be turned overnight into fighter-planes to save their homes.

Unfortunately, an air force—like any other form of expensive life insurance—is appreciated fully only in periods when death is near. The people of Britain, through their representatives in Parliament, have never shown much enthusiasm for air power in peacetime, and it is only the brilliance of our aircraft designers, the courage and skill of our pilots and ground personnel, and the little-deserved protection of Providence that have made it possible for the history of the Royal Air Force to be such a glorious record of achievement.

I

Military flying was pioneered by the French. Having invented the balloon in 1783, they tethered it to a winch and sent it up, complete with an intrepid aeronaut, as an aerial observation post from which every move of an enemy army could be watched and reported. The victory gained by General Jourdan's Moselle army at the Battle of Fleurus, in Belgium, on June 26th, 1794, was said to owe much to reports signalled to the ground by Captain Coutelle, the first-ever military flyer.

Despite such successes, nearly 70 years passed before the British Army would have anything to do with these new-fangled ideas. Finally, in 1863, one of the country's leading balloonists, Henry Coxwell, was commissioned to make a series of ascents at Aldershot, to show how captive balloons might be used for reconnaissance and signalling, and to drop 'aerial torpedoes' on the enemy—a technique he had been the first to demonstrate, in Berlin, in 1848.

On one occasion he was accompanied by Lieut. G. E. Grover and Capt. F. Beaumont of the Royal Engineers, who reported that 'under certain circumstances, the balloon affords means to an army of carrying with it a lofty point of observation.' Bearing in mind that the French army had utilised balloons for this express purpose in the previous century, it was hardly a world-shattering declaration —but another 15 years went by before military experiments with balloons began officially at Woolwich Arsenal in 1878.

Two years later, a balloon section took part in the Aldershot manoeuvres. Further participation in 1882 was judged so successful that the Balloon Equipment Store was transferred from Woolwich to the School of Military Engineering at Chatham, where a small balloon factory, depot and training school were soon established.

At last, in 1884, one hundred and one years after its invention, the balloon went to war with the British army. Three balloons, two officers and 15 other ranks accompanied an expedition to Bechuana-land, after freebooters had hoisted a republican flag at Mafeking and proceeded to carve up the adjacent country. Peace and order were restored without a shot being fired, although it must be admitted that the air detachment did not play a very significant role in the operation.

Mafeking is so high above sea level that the two smaller balloons could not produce sufficient lift to raise a man into the air. The larger model managed to get a single observer off the ground, and the opportunity was taken of giving one of the local chiefs, named Montsiou, a brief taste of tethered flight. Afterwards, he remarked: 'If the first white men who came into this country had brought a thing like that and, having gone up in it before our eyes, had then come down and demanded that we should worship and serve them, we would have done so. The English have indeed great power.'

Recalling this anecdote later in the introductory chapters to his official history of the 1914–18 *War in the Air*, Sir Walter Raleigh commented: 'The chief was right. For any nation to which is entrusted the policing and administration of large tracts of un-civilised country, an air force, civil and military, is an instrument of great power.' These were prophetic words, as we shall see; but it was to be the heavier-than-air aeroplane, rather than the lighter-than-air balloon, which would become the instrument of power.

Balloons accompanied a further expedition to the Sudan in 1885, but they still did not form a recognised part of the Army, and it was only the personal interest of Majors H. Elsdale and J. L. B. Templer which kept military ballooning alive in Britain. Not until 1890 was a Balloon Section established officially as a unit of the Royal Engineers, but after that things moved more rapidly. Within four years, the balloon factory had been moved to South Farn-borough where, after transfer to a better site in 1905, it grew steadily in size and importance, becoming successively His Majesty's Balloon Factory (in 1908), the Army Aircraft Factory, the Royal Aircraft Factory (1912) and finally the Royal Aircraft Establishment, one of the world's greatest aviation research centres.

The South African War of 1899–1902 emphasised both the value and the problems of balloon operation. Successes were achieved by the four sections which saw action, notably in directing the fire of British artillery at Magersfontein and during the battle of Lombard's Kop; but many field commanders were prejudiced against them. There was some excuse for their attitude, as the steel tubes containing compressed hydrogen to inflate the balloons were cumbersome and heavy to transport, the artillery were not properly trained to make full use of the balloons, and the system of signalling by flags left much to be desired, to the extent that the balloonists often failed to attract the attention of the gunners until it was too late for their information to be of any use.

Balloons were also difficult to control in a high wind, but this disadvantage was eliminated when August von Parseval and H. B. von Sigsfeld of Germany invented the sausage-shaped *drachen* or kite balloon with tail-fins to keep it pointed into wind. Balloons of this shape served with the British forces for observation and artillery direction in the first World War, and as anti-aircraft barrage balloons in both World Wars. They were, however, overshadowed completely by later forms of aircraft.

As early as January 1902, the superintendent of the balloon factory, by now Colonel Templer, had visited Paris to report on the airship experiments of Alberto Santos-Dumont. He returned convinced of the military potential of the powered, navigable airship which was free to roam the skies without the limitations of the tethered balloon or of the free balloon, which would drift only where the wind carried it. But so little money was allocated to the factory by the War Office that construction of the first British army airship at Farnborough was not completed until 1907.

Named the *Nulli Secundus*, this sausage-shaped craft was about 120 ft. long and less than 30 ft. in diameter. Powered by a French-built Antoinette engine of 40–50 h.p., it flew at 16 m.p.h. and succeeded in flying from Farnborough to London on October 5th, 1907. After circling St. Paul's Cathedral, it manoeuvred over the grounds of Buckingham Palace before turning for home. In the event, it got no further than the Crystal Palace because of a strong headwind, and *Nulli Secundus* eventually arrived back at Farnborough by road, deflated.

It was the first of a series of successful airships built at Farnborough; but their importance was gradually overshadowed by a different, more practical form of aircraft—the heavier-than-air, fixed-wing aeroplane.

Long before the U.S. services were prepared to recognise the achievement of the Wright brothers in making the first powered, sustained aeroplane flight in December 1903, one of Templer's associates, Colonel J. E. Capper, went to North Carolina to invite the Wrights to continue their experiments in Britain. This might have changed the whole history of aircraft development had the Treasury agreed to finance this transatlantic brain drain in reverse, but it refused to do so and the balloon factory was compelled to utilise its own limited resources.

Chief of these resources was another American pioneer named Samuel Franklin Cody, who had succeeded in interesting the War Office in his man-lifting kites as a more efficient substitute for balloons. He became Chief Instructor in Kiting to the Balloon School in 1906, but was far too energetic to be tied to a single job. He designed the car and power plant of the *Nulli Secundus* airship and was co-pilot to Capper when it made its successful flight to London. He fitted a small engine to one of his kites and flew it successfully in unpiloted form, then set to work on a full-size version.

So it was that the big bamboo-and-canvas biplane known officially as British Army Aeroplane No. 1, which made the first officially-recognised aeroplane flight in the U.K. on October 16th, 1908, was built at Farnborough by an American citizen.

Being a former fighter of Indians, hunter of buffalo and manager of a travelling wild west show, Cody had a habit of riding round Farnborough on a richly-saddled white horse, with a revolver at his hip and long hair flowing from beneath a wide-brimmed stetson hat. However, such eccentricities were not new to the men of the Balloon Factory, as Templer had often taken his wife shopping in a caravan hauled by a ten-ton traction engine.

This may seem irrelevant, but it is not. The whole story of Britain's fighting services is permeated by the contributions of men who were larger-than-life, not only in their habits but in their thoughts. Just as frequently, it records the ineptitude of politicians of every party—like those who, in 1909, decided that the £2,500 spent on financing the aviation activities of Cody and his colleagues at Farnborough was so exorbitant that all work on aeroplanes had to stop forthwith. They seemed to regard as inconsequential the fact that Germany had spent about £400,000 on military aeronautics by that time—mainly in connection with the giant metal-framed airships designed by Graf Ferdinand von Zeppelin.

The situation in Britain improved a little in October 1910, when the scope of the Balloon Section of the Royal Engineers was extended 'to afford opportunities for aeroplaning.' By this time the Balloon School had been separated from the Factory. Capper continued to command the former; Superintendent of the Factory was Mervyn O'Gorman, who placed fresh emphasis on the importance of a scientific approach to aeronautical research and development. He gathered round him a small band of highly-skilled designers and engineers, headed by Frederick Green who came from the Daimler company as Engineer in Charge of Design.

Officially, there was still nothing to design, as the War Office ban on aeroplane work at Farnborough remained in force. However, O'Gorman was allowed to buy for £400 an existing aeroplane and take on its young builder as a designer/test pilot. The name of the young man was Geoffrey de Havilland and it was not long before he began to display the genius that was to make him one of the great figures of British aviation.

In December 1910, the month that he joined Green's small staff, the War Office sent to the factory for repair an experimental Blériot monoplane that had earned itself the nickname 'Man-Killer.'

With a cunning born of frustration, the designers requested official permission to reconstruct the aircraft. This was given, and when the Blériot re-emerged, with the Factory designation S.E.1, it had been transformed from a tractor monoplane to a tail-first pusher biplane. The only vestige of the original aircraft that remained was the 60 h.p. E.N.V. engine!

A few months later, a Voisin pusher biplane was 'repaired' so thoroughly, under the leadership of Green and de Havilland, that it was transformed into a completely new type of tractor biplane known as the B.E.1. Even the 60 h.p. Wolseley engine inherited from the Voisin was soon replaced by a Renault of similar power. This ran so quietly by comparison with the more usual rotary engines of the period that the B.E.1 became known as the 'Silent Aeroplane'.

It remained in service for more than three years, during which it survived many mishaps and repairs and was used for a wide variety of experiments, including tests with one of the earliest airborne radio transmitters.

Sir Walter Raleigh wrote of the B.E.1: 'The first machine of its type, it outlived generations of its successors, and before it yielded to fate had become the revered grandfather of the whole brood of factory aeroplanes.'

The change in War Office thinking which gave birth to this brood came on February 28th, 1911, when an Army Order was issued proclaiming that, on April 1st that year, the Balloon Section of the Royal Engineers would be expanded into an Air Battalion. This was to comprise an H.Q. at South Farnborough, No. 1 (Airship) Company, also at Farnborough, and No. 2 (Aeroplane) Company at Larkhill on Salisbury Plain.

So came into being the first British military unit equipped entirely with heavier-than-air craft. It is interesting to note that the qualifications laid down for pilots included possession of an aviator's certificate, previous experience in aeronautics, good map-reading and field sketching, not less than two years' service, being a good sailor and having an aptitude for mechanics.

To a degree these made sense. Nobody foresaw much use for military aviation beyond reconnaissance, hence the need for good map-reading and sketching. The poor stability of aeroplanes of the period offered some reason for believing that pilots ought to be good sailors; while the frequency of engine failures and forced landings made mechanical ability essential. The main drawback was, perhaps, the requirement that would-be pilots should already have gained their aviator's certificate, as this limited the field to those who had the cash, as well as the initiative and courage, to take flying lessons. However, the War Office undertook to repay £75 of the cost of such training on acceptance of a pilot for service with the Air Battalion.

Commandant of the Battalion was Major Sir Alexander Bannerman, with Captain E. M. Maitland in charge of the Airship Company and Captain J. D. B. Fulton commanding the Aeroplane Company. By the Summer of 1911, the latter had six Bristol Boxkite biplanes (four with 50 h.p. Gnome engines, two with 60 h.p. Renault), a somewhat-battered Henri Farman (50 h.p. Gnome), a reconstructed Howard Wright biplane and a 70 h.p. Blériot XXI monoplane which belonged personally to one of the pilots.

Such was the enthusiasm of the Aeroplane Company that, when the Army's autumn manoeuvres were cancelled, it asked permission to test its capabilities by flying to what would have been the air bases for the exercise, at Hardwicke, near Cambridge, and Thetford in Norfolk. Only two aeroplanes completed the round trip unscathed. Two pilots wrote off their aircraft completely; another crashed two aeroplanes on successive days.

After such a dismal performance, there was some justification for the War Office's belief that it would save money and get better aeroplanes if it standardised on types designed and built in its own, newly-renamed Army Aircraft Factory at Farnborough. Fortunately, this intention was never fully implemented, but even in diminished form it nearly brought disaster to Britain's air forces when they eventually went to war.

The reason was, paradoxically, that the Factory succeeded too well in giving the Army what it wanted. With the entire emphasis on reconnaissance, Green and de Havilland evolved from their B.E.1 'Silent Aeroplane' the improved B.E.2/2a/2b series. One of their colleagues, Edward Busk, specialised in research into aircraft stability and control problems. To investigate his theories in the air, he took flying training and, with great courage, flew a B.E.2a beyond its safe limits of controllability on several occasions.

When convinced that he could produce a far more stable aircraft, he had his innovations embodied in a new variant of the basic design, known as the B.E.2c. This retained the fuselage, under-carriage and power plant of the B.E.2b, but introduced new wings, with a marked degree of stagger (i.e. the top wing was placed in advance of the lower one) and with ailerons instead of the former wing-warping control system. A fixed tail-fin was added, forward of the rudder, and a new tailplane was fitted, in a lower position on the fuselage than the original type.

The B.E.2c proved to be incredibly stable.  On one occasion, Major (later Air Vice Marshal Sir) Sefton Brancker climbed to a height of 2,000 feet over Farnborough in the prototype, pointed the aircraft in the direction of Netheravon and did not touch the controls again until he was down to only 20 feet above the ground at his destination. He spent his time in flight writing a reconnaissance report of the countryside passing beneath him.

Here, it seemed, was the perfect reconnaissance aircraft, and it was ordered in huge numbers by the War Office.  The fact that an inherently stable aeroplane is insufficiently manoeuvrable to survive in air combat mattered not at all, at the time, as aircraft did not carry guns.  But within a year of the outbreak of the first World War, the Germans put into service the Fokker monoplane, armed with a machine-gun, and the B.E.2c's were destroyed in such numbers that they are remembered today not for their qualities but as 'Fokker Fodder.'

Had Farnborough been the only design centre for British military aircraft, the outlook for our air forces might have been very bleak, but for once in history an inter-service rivalry was to have a happy outcome.

To see why, we must go back to 1911 and the start of British naval flying.  The Admiralty's lukewarm interest was chilled on September 24th that year when its first aircraft—an airship with the unpromising nickname of *Mayfly*—broke its back before making even a single flight.  Airship experiments were discontinued and the officers, headed by Captain (later Rear Admiral Sir) Murray Sueter, who had been allocated to the programme were returned to general duties.

There was, however, a small bunch of naval aviators at Eastchurch in Kent, which was then the home of both the Royal Aero Club's flying activities and the Short brothers' factory.

Back in February 1911, Mr. (later Sir) Francis McClean had offered the loan of two Short biplanes to enable naval officers to learn to fly at Eastchurch, provided the Admiralty would pay for their running expenses and maintenance.  When his fellow Aero Club member G. B. Cockburn offered his services freely as an instructor, their Lordships could hardly refuse such generosity.  It was made clear to would-be naval pilots that if they volunteered for training they would lose seniority and could never expect to be given command of a ship—despite which there were over 200 applicants.

The four who eventually found themselves at Eastchurch were Lieutenants R. Gregory, C. R. Samson and A. M. Longmore of the Royal Navy and Lieutenant E. L. Gerrard of the Royal Marine Light Infantry. All qualified for their aviator's certificate within six weeks, during which time they also completed a course of aircraft engineering in the Short works. In October, Samson persuaded the Admiralty not only to buy the two aircraft but to send a dozen naval ratings to Eastchurch to form the nucleus of a flying school.

Meanwhile, the British government and people had received a grim warning of growing German militarism. The newspapers on Monday July 3rd, 1911 told how Germany had decided to use recent disturbances in the northern part of Morocco as an excuse for a show of force at the port of Agadir, hundreds of miles away on the Atlantic coast. Out of the blue, the gunboat *Panther* arrived there 'to protect German interests', although there were no Europeans in Agadir and Germany had neither interests nor commerce to protect in that part of Morocco. The crisis was ended by the treaty of November 4th; but many people in Britain felt that the next show of strength might be much nearer home, on a much larger scale.

Taking stock of its defence forces, the government discovered, *inter alia*, that the Air Battalion had one or two small experimental airships with well-worn gasbags and a few airworthy aeroplanes suitable for little else but training. There were thought to be 'eleven actual flying men' in the Army and eight in the Navy.

Time was running out fast. The Prime Minister, Herbert Asquith, asked the Committee of Imperial Defence to look into the whole question of naval and military aviation and suggest measures by which Britain could create an efficient air force. Within weeks the government were informed of the Committee's recommendations, which were simple and to the point. They called primarily for the establishment of a Royal Flying Corps, with separate Military and Naval Wings; a Reserve; retention of the Royal Aircraft Factory at Farnborough; and the setting up of a Central Flying School at which all pilots would be trained for both Wings.

The Royal Flying Corps (R.F.C.) was constituted by a Royal Warrant on April 13th, 1912 and on May 13th it absorbed the old Air Battalion and its reserve. The sum of £308,000 was voted by Parliament to set the service on its feet—an amount which would not buy even a single fighter aircraft today.

Brilliant though the concept had been, it was doomed to failure from the start, by the very nature of the partners in the enterprise. The Navy had always set great store on personal initiative; the Army ran on regulations. The Navy was a technical service in which equipment was the prime factor and the personnel simply a means of operating it more efficiently. In the Army, the soldier was the prime factor and the equipment only a means of making him more efficient. The Navy's task was to sink ships, the Army's to kill men.

Psychological differences were reflected in differing approaches to aviation. The Military Wing concentrated on reconnaissance and selected the Factory-designed B.E.2 series as its main operational equipment, supplemented by aircraft purchased in France. The Naval Wing, encouraged by the First Lord of the Admiralty, Winston Churchill, pioneered the operation of aircraft from ships under way, made successfully the first launch of a torpedo from an aircraft in flight, conducted scientific bomb-dropping experiments by throwing potatoes overboard from a flying-boat and even began to think in terms of strategic bombing of enemy targets. They preferred their own flying school at Eastchurch to the new Central Flying School at Upavon, and they preferred the products of private companies like Short and Sopwith to the standardised aeroplanes designed at Farnborough.

The inevitable, if somewhat unconstitutional, result was a pronouncement on July 1st, 1914 that the Naval Wing would in future be known as the Royal Naval Air Service (R.N.A.S.), followed by a gradual severing of the remaining links between the two air services.

Both had their share of 'characters'—like Charles Rumney Samson, Commander, R.N. One of the four original naval aviators and first man in the world to fly from a moving ship, he was a jaunty, bearded little man with unlimited courage and limited patience. On the outbreak of war in August 1914, he was despatched to Belgium as commander of the Eastchurch squadron of the R.N.A.S., to carry out reconnaissance for a Marine Brigade, using ten aeroplanes (of six different types) and a small number of armoured motor cars.

The adventures of Samson's 'Dunkirk Force' deserve a book to themselves. They culminated in a strategic bombing raid by two 80 h.p. Sopwith Tabloids, one of which, piloted by Flt. Lieut. R. L. G. Marix, deposited its tiny 20 lb bombs so accurately that they destroyed a huge airship shed at Düsseldorf, complete with the new and secret Zeppelin Z.IX inside.

So impressed was Captain Murray Sueter, then Director of the Air Department of the Admiralty, that he went to see Frederick Handley Page and asked him to produce for the R.N.A.S. 'a bloody paralyser of an aeroplane.' This somewhat sketchy specification took shape in due course as the 0/100, sire of the whole world-beating succession of British heavy bombers.

While the R.N.A.S. pioneered strategic bombing, learned to operate from warships, evolved the first true aircraft carriers, made the first successful torpedo attacks from the air against enemy ships, mastered the Zeppelin and brought their private enterprise fighters and bombers to the aid of the hard-pressed R.F.C. squadrons on the Western Front, the erstwhile Military Wing was also developing into a proud fighting service. The man most responsible for this was Hugh Trenchard, remembered now as Marshal of the Royal Air Force Viscount Trenchard, the crusader for and architect of British air power.

There was little hint of the crusader in the Captain Trenchard who had been shunted into a quiet staff job, to work out the remaining years before retirement, after recovering from near-fatal wounds in the South African War and a deadly bout of fever in Nigeria. But, in fact, his real career was only beginning.

When told in July 1912 that he might qualify for an appointment at the Central Flying School if he obtained an aviator's certificate before the end of that month, he hurried down to Brooklands to see his friend 'Tommy' Sopwith and was soon airborne in a tired old Henri Farman biplane. Complete with his certificate, he volunteered for the first pilot training course at the C.F.S., where he soon became Station Staff Officer.

This raised a slight problem in that he had not yet qualified for his military 'wings' at that time. However, on looking up the duties of an S.S.O., he discovered that they included setting examination papers, arranging and invigilating examinations, correcting papers and either passing or failing the candidates. So he set himself a flying and ground examination, was the invigilating officer, corrected and assessed his own paper and awarded himself his 'wings.'

In September 1913, Trenchard became Assistant Commandant of the C.F.S. Eleven months later, he found himself with a row of almost empty sheds, a few officers and men who were unfit for service overseas and some decrepit aircraft unfit for anything at all. Every man and every aircraft that could fly had been wafted over to France as part of the British Expeditionary Force. They totalled 105 officers, 63 aeroplanes and 95 motor vehicles.

Trenchard was given the task of creating a new air force out of what was left in England, and of ensuring sufficient reserves to keep the squadrons in France up to strength. This he did to the best of his ability in three months before he was posted to France to command No. 1 Wing of the R.F.C.

In August 1915 he was promoted to command the entire R.F.C. on active service. It was a critical moment, for the whole character of military aviation was changing with the arrival on the Western Front of the first Fokker monoplane fighters. Up to that time, the reconnaissance aircraft of both sides had been able to perform their vital task without serious hindrance. Isolated successes had been achieved by shooting at them from other aircraft with revolvers, shot-guns, carbines, and machine-guns mounted in such a way that the bullets would pass outside the arc of the propeller; but the real fighter-plane was born when Anthony Fokker invented a synchronisation gear that enabled bullets from a machine-gun to be fired between the propeller blades of a single-seat 'scout'. Soon his little monoplanes began driving the British and French aircraft from the sky, the B.E.2's suffering particularly heavy casualties.

Under the guidance of Trenchard and through the genius of British designers, who produced a wonderful new series of fighters, including the D.H.2, F.E.2b, Camel and S.E.5, the R.F.C. gradually regained the initiative; but the experience of the 'Fokker Scourge' had convinced many people in England that the whole concept of Britain's air forces, and the policy of equipping the R.F.C. with aircraft designed at the Royal Aircraft Factory, was wrong.

An Air Board was established in 1916 to discuss matters of general policy in relation to the air, to recommend types of machines required, and to co-ordinate research and the supply of equipment to the two services. It was a step in the right direction; but when German bombers attacked London in daylight in June and July 1917 there was such a public outcry that General Smuts was given the job of examining the whole structure of Britain's air defences and organisation.

His report was ready by mid-August 1917. Its main recommendations were that the Air Board should be expanded into a full Air Ministry, and that the Royal Flying Corps and Royal Naval Air Service should be amalgamated. So, *per ardua*, was conceived the Royal Air Force.

# Chapter Two

# Foundations for a Castle

*The word Trenchard spells out confidence in the R.A.F. . . . . We think of him as immense, not by what he says, for he is as near as can be inarticulate . . . and not by what he writes, for he makes the least use of what must be the world's worst handwriting—but just by what he is. He knows; and by virtue of this pole-star of knowledge he steers through all the ingenuity and cleverness and hesitations of the little men who help or hinder him.*

T. E. Lawrence, 'The Mint', 1922

THE BILL sanctioning establishment of an Air Ministry as a Department of State was passed by Parliament and received Royal Assent on November 29th, 1917. Lord Rothermere became Secretary of State and President of the Air Council, in which the final authority of the Air Ministry was vested. There was only one possible choice for the leader of the new service and the announcement that the first Chief of the Air Staff would be Major-General Sir Hugh Trenchard, K.C.B., D.S.O., caused no surprise. His Deputy was Rear-Admiral Mark Kerr, C.B., R.N.

To make the transition as smooth as possible, the re-amalgamation of the R.F.C. and R.N.A.S. was planned as a gradual process and the Royal Air Force did not come into being until April 1st, 1918. It bore no comparison to the tiny force despatched to France in August 1914. Britain's aircraft industry had grown so rapidly that it delivered an average of 2,668 aircraft per month in 1918, enabling the R.A.F. to field a front-line strength of 2,630 aircraft by mid-year. Of these, 1,736 were on the Western Front, 104 on the Italian Front, 41 on the Macedonian Front, 269 in the Middle East and 144 in the Mediterranean, with 336 allocated to home defence.

Over 35 per cent of the total were classed as corps reconnaissance or two-seat reconnaissance fighter aircraft, which underlines the fact that the primary tasks of the British air force continued to be observation of the enemy, on behalf of the Army and Navy, and directing the fire of Allied artillery. It was unglamorous work, calling for a high degree of courage.

Writing of the Factory-designed aircraft which succeeded the B.E.2's, in his standard reference work on *British Aeroplanes 1914–18*, J. M. Bruce comments: 'Those who flew in France during the years 1917 and 1918 are not likely to forget the seemingly ever-present R.E.8, flying its stolid, elliptical course, and trailing a wake of anti-aircraft shell-bursts behind it. That it did much good work in this way is to the credit of the pilots and observers who flew it. The R.E.8 was given to them without choice of alternative: in it they did their duty.'

Great progress was made in developing more effective equipment for reconnaissance aircraft during the first World War. Accurate and prompt direction and correction of artillery fire would have been impossible without steady improvements in air-to-ground wireless telegraphy, and the efficiency of reconnaissance operations was increased enormously by R.F.C. pioneering of air photography. As early as March 1915, an experimental photographic section under Lieut. J. T. C. Moore-Brabazon (later Lord Brabazon of Tara), attached to the 1st Wing in France, had produced the first specialised air camera. From that time, British troops were able to go into action with a complete knowledge of the enemy's hidden defences, shown on maps based on air photographs: and in a single week before the great German offensive on the Somme, in March 1918, no fewer than 10,441 photographs were taken to warn and aid the Allied troops who had to bear the brunt of the onslaught.

Books and films about the first World War pay scant attention to the work of the reconnaissance squadrons. This is understandable, as something of the old 'knights in shining armour' aura surrounded the fighter squadrons, with their garishly-decorated aircraft, piloted by larger-than-life 'aces' like von Richthofen, Guynemer, Mannock and Rickenbacker. But it should never be forgotten that the main task of the fighter squadrons was not to destroy enemy fighters but to prevent enemy reconnaissance aircraft from supplying information that could make the difference between victory or defeat in the grim struggle on the ground.

They did not always have things their own way. For example, on August 16th, 1917, during the battle of Langemarck, an R.E.8 of No. 7 Squadron was attacked by two German Albatros fighters while engaged in photography. Its observer promptly shot down one of the enemy, at which the other dived away. Later that day, another aircraft from the same squadron was set upon by eight Albatros. A 60-round burst of fire from close range disposed of one of the enemy fighters; the others turned for home.

All too often, however, the reconnaissance aircraft were the losers: as on April 13th, 1917, when six R.E.8's of No. 59 Squadron set out on an early-morning photographic sortie. Two carried cameras, the others being intended as escorts. Despite the limited fighting capabilities of the R.E.8, this was considered adequate, as there were known to be fighter patrols of six F.E.2d's, three Spads and the Bristol Fighters of No. 48 Squadron in the area. Unfortunately, two of the F.E.'s were shot down and the others dispersed; the Spads were late on the scene and the Bristol Fighters never caught sight of the R.E.8's, all of which fell in a matter of minutes before the guns of von Richthofen's squadron.

Bearing in mind that the British Sopwith Camel alone destroyed 1,294 enemy aircraft in air combat in 1917–18, it is sobering to recall in these days of 1,500 m.p.h., 20-ton fighters that its engine developed less power than that of a modern two-seat lightplane trainer like the Cherokee and that its maximum speed was a mere 115 m.p.h. The weight of a Sopwith Pup fighter, complete with pilot, gun and fuel, was only 1,225 lb—about the same as the four air-to-air missiles carried by a Sea Vixen today—and the cost of its airframe was £710 18s. By comparison, the airframes of some modern combat aircraft cost more than their weight in pure gold.

Altogether, 1,120 of the R.A.F.'s first-line aircraft in June 1918 were single-seat fighters. Only 422 were bombers, of which a mere 10 were long-range heavy bombers; but the importance of these aircraft was out of all proportion to their numbers.

Apart from a few early efforts by the R.N.A.S., like the Tabloid raid on Düsseldorf, most British bombing was tactical, in direct support of the land, air or sea battles. The enemy, on the other hand, began an airship offensive against the United Kingdom on the night of January 19th–20th, 1915, and kept up this form of attack, at mounting cost, until August 5th, 1918. In 51 raids, German airships dropped 196½ tons of bombs, killing 557 people and injuring another 1,358. Estimated monetary damage caused in these attacks was £1,527,585.

This may seem a feeble effort by comparison with the mighty Anglo-American air offensive against Germany in World War II, but it must be remembered that civilian populations had never before been subjected to this type of ordeal and the effect on morale was considerable.

By mid-1917, the Zeppelin had been mastered to a degree by fighter aircraft firing incendiary ammunition. This is reflected in statistics which show that of 62 operational Zeppelins put into service, 19 were shot down, 11 wrecked by bad weather and 11 destroyed by accident or bombing in their sheds. That is why Germany put increasing emphasis on the use of long-range bomber aeroplanes of the kind which, as we have seen, caused a major uproar by attacking London in full view of the populace, without apparent hindrance, in June and July 1917.

If all had gone according to plan, the R.N.A.S. would by 1916 have been engaged on a major strategic bombing campaign against Germany; but it suffered repeated frustrations. The original plan to open the offensive with 20 Sopwith 1½-Strutters, 15 Short bombers and 20 1½-Strutter escort fighters, deployed by No. 3 Wing at Luxeuil, near Nancy, was abandoned when the R.F.C. pleaded for additional aircraft with which to support the army at the Battle of the Somme. Sixty-two Sopwiths were transferred to the R.F.C. by September 1916, at the expense of No. 3 Wing.

Between October 12th and the Spring of 1917, No. 3 Wing made effective, if intermittent, attacks on German industrial targets, side-by-side with French squadrons. Then, once more, the R.F.C. asked for naval aid, which was forthcoming to such a degree that No. 3 Wing had to be disbanded.

The resumption of strategic bombing raids on Germany was in direct retaliation for aeroplane attacks against England. By this time, a powerful new weapon was available in the shape of the Handley Page 0/100—Murray Sueter's 'bloody paralyser'. Whereas the Short bomber carried only eight 65 lb bombs, the 0/100 could take as many as sixteen 112-pounders. A squadron of these mighty aircraft was sent to join the 41st Wing, formed at Ochey, near Nancy, in company with No. 100 Squadron (F.E.2b night bombers) and No. 55 Squadron (D.H.4 day bombers). Later, they were reinforced by Nos. 99 and 104 Squadrons, equipped with D.H.9's. Despite a severe winter, these units—renamed the VIII Brigade in February—made 142 raids on enemy targets between October 11th, 1917 and June 5th, 1918.

By this latter date there had been a major change in the high command of the newly-formed R.A.F. Finding himself unable to work with Rothermere, Trenchard had resigned as Chief of the Air Staff and had been replaced by Major-General Sir Frederick Sykes. This was far less disastrous than it might have been. In May 1918 the government decided that VIII Brigade had proved so effective that it should be expanded into an Independent Force with the sole task of carrying out an extended and sustained bombing offensive against German munition factories, and Trenchard was appointed to command it.

The Independent Force was the first unit of its kind to operate without any responsibility for—or without being under the control of—troops on the ground. The five months which he spent at its head confirmed Trenchard's views on the extreme importance of air attack, compared with passive defence, as a means of victory in war.

No fewer than four squadrons of big twin-engined Handley Page o/100 and improved o/400 bombers formed the heart of the night-bombing force at his disposal, backed up by two squadrons of D.H.9's, one of D.H.9a's with American-built Liberty engines, one of F.E.2b's, one of D.H.4's and one of Sopwith Camel fighters.

The Camels were essential to protect the day bombers, as the Germans devoted more and more effort into trying to halt the onslaught of the Independent Force. They might as well have tried Canute-like to turn back the ocean tide. Even when a forma-tion of British bombers lost the majority of its aircraft, the surviving pilots struck back again at the same targets.

Careful planning went into the offensive. Primary targets included poison gas plants, aeroplane factories and aero-engine factories, with railways and blast furnaces as the most important alternatives if a main objective could not be reached. Altogether, 550 tons of bombs were dropped in five months, 160 tons by day and 390 tons by night. Of the total, 220 tons were unloaded over enemy aero-dromes, to such good effect that attacks on Allied aerodromes became negligible and not a single aeroplane was destroyed by enemy bombing during the lifetime of the Independent Force.

Of equal importance was the large number of photo-reconnaiss-ance sorties flown by the Force, usually by single aircraft at great height; for these revealed the extent of damage caused to enemy targets and ensured the most economical use of the bombing effort.

Had the war not ended when it did, the Germans would have been subjected to even heavier attacks, for there was assembling in Britain the first squadron of Handley Page V/1500 four-engined bombers—great even by today's standards—each able to carry up to thirty 250 lb bombs. But the war did end, on November 11th, 1918, and within a matter of months the R.A.F. was reduced from a tremendous force of 188 combat squadrons and 15 flights—made up of 291,170 officers and men and 22,647 aircraft—to a mere 33 squadrons. Once again it was Trenchard, re-appointed Chief of the Air Staff, who had the task of rebuilding the remnants into an efficient air force.

He did so against bitter opposition from the War Office and Admiralty, who played every card in their hand to divide and regain control of Britain's air forces. Encouraged by Winston Churchill, who combined the duties of Secretary of State for Air and Secretary of State for War, he set out his ideas in a document dated December 11th, 1919, entitled officially *Cmd. 467. Permanent Organisation of the Royal Air Force—Note by the Secretary of State for Air on a Scheme Outlined by the Chief of the Air Staff*, but usually known simply as 'Trenchard's White Paper'. Published by the Stationery Office, it cost just one penny, for which the public were able to read the most remarkable and far-sighted piece of constructive planning in the annals of air power.

He began by reminding all concerned that: 'The problem confronting us—the problem of forming the Royal Air Force on a peace basis differs in many essentials from that which confronts the older services. The Royal Air Force was formed by the amalgamation of the Royal Flying Corps and the Royal Naval Air Service, and one may say, broadly speaking, that the whole Service was practically a war creation on a temporary basis, without any possibility of taking into account that it was going to remain on a permanent basis. The personnel with few exceptions was enlisted for the duration of the war, and put through an intensive but necessarily hurried course of training. Material was created in vast quantities, but rapid development often rendered it obsolete almost before it had reached the stage of bulk production. The accommodation provided had perforce to be of an entirely temporary character. The force may in fact be compared to the prophet Jonah's gourd. The necessities of war created it in a night, but the economies of peace have to a large extent caused it to wither in a day, and we are now faced with the necessity of replacing it with a plant of deeper root. As in nature, however, decay fosters growth, and the new plant has a fruitful soil from which to spring.

'The principle to be kept in mind in forming the framework of the Air Service is that in future the main portion of it will consist in an Independent Force, together with Service personnel required of carrying out Aeronautical Research.

'In addition, there will be a small part of it specially trained for work with the Navy, and a small part specially trained for work with the Army, these two small portions probably becoming, in the future, an arm of the older services.

'It may be that the main portion, the Independent Air Force, will grow larger and larger, and become more and more the predominating factor in all types of warfare.

'Governing principles. In planning the formation of the peace Royal Air Force it has been assumed that no need will arise for some years at least for anything in the nature of general mobilisation. It has been possible therefore to concentrate attention on providing for the needs of the moment as far as they can be foreseen and on laying the foundations of a highly-trained and efficient force which, though not capable of expansion in its present form, can be made so without any drastic alteration should necessity arise in years to come. Broadly speaking, the principle has been to reduce service squadrons to the minimum considered essential for our garrisons overseas with a very small number in the United Kingdom as a reserve, and to concentrate the whole of the remainder of our resources on perfecting the training of officers and men.'

Trenchard recommended that the few squadrons that the Air Force possessed in 1919 should be allocated to Home Defence, the Middle East, India, the Navy and the Army. Realising that, with the 'war to end wars' newly won, there would be no money for new aeroplanes, he continued: 'We now come to that on which the whole future of the Royal Air Force depends, namely, the training of its officers and men. The present need is not, under existing conditions, the creation of the full number of squadrons we may eventually require to meet strategical needs, but it is first and foremost the making of a sound framework on which to build a service, which while giving us now the few essential service squadrons, adequately trained and equipped, will be capable of producing whatever time may show to be necessary in the future.

'Before explaining our proposals in detail it is necessary to lay down certain postulates.

'Firstly, to make an Air Force worthy of the name, we must create an Air Force spirit, or rather foster this spirit which undoubtedly existed in a high degree during the war, by every means in our power. Suggestions have been made that we should rely on the older services to train our cadets and Staff officers. To do so would make the creation of an Air Force spirit an impossibility apart from the practical objection, among others, that the existing naval and military cadet and staff colleges are not provided with aerodromes or situated in localities in any way suited for flying training.

'Secondly, we must use every endeavour to eliminate flying accidents, both during training and subsequently.  This end can only be secured by ensuring that the training of our mechanics in the multiplicity of trades necessitated by a highly technical service, is as thorough as it can be made.  The best way to do this is to enlist the bulk of our skilled ranks as boys and train them ourselves.  This has the added advantage that it will undoubtedly foster the Air Force spirit on which so much depends.

'Thirdly, it is not sufficient to make the Air Force officer a chauffeur and nothing more.

'Technical experts are required for the development of the science of aeronautics, still in its infancy.  Navigation, meteorology, photography and wireless are primary necessities if the Air Force is to be more than a means of conveyance, and the first two are requisite for safety, even on the chauffeur basis.'

The whole theme of Trenchard's master plan was one of purposeful farsightedness, detailing his proposals for the provision of a Cadet College for officers at Cranwell, in Lincolnshire; a scheme for short-service commissions;  the provision of a school for flying instructors—evolved from the Central Flying School—and of an Air Force Staff College;  and, of prime importance for the future expansion of a technical force, the initiation of the apprenticeship scheme, where boys could undergo a course of three years' training in technical subjects before passing into the ranks.  It eventually became an honour to be referred to as a 'Halton Brat'.

These were the salient points of Trenchard's plan.  It remained to be seen whether or not it would be accepted by an economy-minded government.  Trenchard himself commented simply:  'I have laid the foundations for a castle; if nobody builds anything bigger than a cottage on them, it will at least be a very good cottage.'

# Chapter Three

# Wars without End

---

*Woe is me, that I am constrained to dwell with Mesech:*
*and to have my habitation among the tents of Kedar.*
*My soul hath long dwelt among them that are enemies*
*unto peace.*
*I labour for peace, but when I speak unto them thereof:*
*they make them ready to battle.*

*Psalm* 120

TRENCHARD WAS RIGHT in his assumption that no need for anything in the nature of a general mobilisation of Britain's armed forces would arise for some years. The two decades from 1919 to 1939 are remembered generally as the 'between-wars years'; and yet, for the Royal Air Force, nothing could be farther from the truth, for there was no period in the 'twenties or 'thirties when it was without a war to fight somewhere in the world.

Much of its warfare was centred in the Middle East, where the 20th century tribes were no more peaceable than their ancestors, the Mesech and Kedar, whom the Psalmist found so objectionable. There was, however, one campaign in a very different part of the world, which can be regarded as an offshoot of the first World War but did not end with the Armistice of November 1918.

The signing of a peace treaty between Germany and Russia, in March 1918, had put the Allies in a difficult position. At all costs, the enemy U-boat force had to be prevented from setting up bases in Russia's Arctic ports of Archangel and Murmansk. It was equally important to keep the resources of Western Siberia out of German hands, and to extricate, through Vladivostock, as many as possible of the 92,000 newly-independent Czechoslovakian troops in Russia, so that they could be transferred to the Western Front. So, in May 1918, General Poole was sent to Murmansk to organise a North Russian Expeditionary Force. Before long, R.A.F. units, equipped with D.H.4 and D.H.9 day bombers, Camel fighters and Fairey, Short and Sopwith seaplanes, were providing valuable support for both the Northern force and other Allied units in South Russia.

The aircraft carrier *Vindictive* joined them in July 1919, primarily to prevent the Bolshevik fleet from leaving Kronstadt for operations against Finland, Estonia and other non-Bolshevik states.

In trying to stem the creation of Communist Russia, the Allies were facing an impossible task. It was decided towards the end of 1919 to evacuate the Northern forces and concentrate on holding the South. Local successes were achieved, as when the Camels of No. 47 Squadron, working in partnership with cavalry, caught a division of enemy troops advancing over the Steppes towards Tsaritsin in October 1919, and inflicted heavy casualties by repeated low-level attacks. But eight months later victory was conceded to the Bolsheviks and the R.A.F. withdrew from Russian territory.

What is not generally known is that the technique of close support, as practised so successfully by No. 47 Squadron, was pioneered by Britain's air forces, on May 3rd, 1917, during the third battle of the Scarpe in France. On learning that German troops were massing for a counter-attack, five Sopwith 1½-Strutters of No. 43 Squadron had raked the enemy with fire from both their front and rear guns, flying only 50 to 300 ft. above the ground.

Shortly afterwards, four more aircraft from the same squadron repeated the tactic, to such good effect that the counter-attack never took place. No aircraft were lost and one pilot commented afterwards: 'The chief danger we had to face was from our artillery barrage. When we shut off our engines for a moment we could clearly hear our own shells rumbling past our ears with a noise that sounded like a succession of trains passing through a tunnel.'

The official history of the war recorded that No. 43 Squadron 'can be said to have definitely established this novel development in the employment of aeroplanes directly to assist troops on the ground; operating in fact as "tanks of the air".' The technique was exploited fully at the battle of Messines a few weeks later and, as in the case of strategic bombing, Britain's air forces have continued to use to good effect the technique they evolved, right up to the present time.

They were given plenty of opportunities to keep in practice in the Middle East. Trenchard had no difficulty in persuading Churchill that Egypt ought to become the keystone of the entire post-war deployment of R.A.F. combat units, because of its comparative nearness to Britain, its equable climate and its central position on the world's trade routes. The romance of aircraft patrolling the vast deserts which flanked the nation's ocean life-lines to the Far East appealed greatly to the Secretary of State, and he approved the plan for basing seven squadrons in Egypt by 1920–21, to be followed by a training wing and schools of air pilotage and gunnery by 1922–23.

Eight squadrons were to be based in India and three in Mesopotamia (now Iraq), with seaplane flights at Malta and Alexandria and afloat in a carrier in the Mediterranean. Thus, of the total of 33 R.A.F. squadrons, including eight in process of formation, in March 1920, more than half were in the Middle East. At home there were twelve squadrons: five with the Inland Area (including three in process of formation) and five with the Coastal Area (including two in process of formation). Two others were in Ireland and one on the Rhine. No increase was contemplated, the main emphasis being on building the squadrons to peak strength and efficiency, as specified in Trenchard's 'White Paper'.

Many of the functions of the former R.N.A.S. were vested in the Coastal Area squadrons. For co-operation with the Fleet there were to be formed, eventually, three aeroplane and two seaplane squadrons, a start being made with a reconnaissance and spotting squadron, half a torpedo squadron, and single flights of fighters, flying-boats and seaplanes. How this 'Cinderella' force was transformed eventually into the Fleet Air Arm is told in the next chapter.

Build-up of the Middle East air forces began only five months after the Armistice, in April 1919, when No. 58 Squadron began the move from France to Egypt with its Handley Page 0/400's. They were followed quickly by two more 0/400 squadrons (Nos. 214 and 216—formerly R.N.A.S. Squadrons 14 and 16 respectively), one squadron of D.H.9 day bombers (No. 206) and one of Sopwith Snipe fighters (No. 80). Simultaneously, two squadrons of Bristol Fighters (Nos. 20 and 48) and one of D.H.9a's (No. 99) were sent to India and one squadron of R.E.8's (No. 6) to Mesopotamia.

It was not the first time that an 0/400 had been seen in the Middle East. A single example had been attached to No. 1 Squadron of the Australian Flying Corps in Palestine and had served well in both the bomber and transport rôles in support of the Arab forces led by Col. T. E. Lawrence (Lawrence of Arabia). In particular, it had wrecked Turkish communications by dropping sixteen 112 lb bombs on the Turks' main telephone exchange at El Affule on September 19th, 1918, on the eve of General Allenby's final big offensive. The pilot was Captain Ross Smith who, with his brother, later made the first flight between Britain and Australia in a Vimy.

The effect of this large aircraft on the Arabs' morale was recorded vividly by Lawrence in *The Seven Pillars of Wisdom*: 'At Um el Surab, the Handley stood majestic on the grass, with Bristols and 9a, like fledglings beneath its spread of wings. Round it admired the Arabs, saying: "Indeed, and at last, they have sent us THE aeroplane, of which these things were foals." Before night, rumours of Feisal's resource went over Jebel Druse and the hollow of Hauran, telling people that the balance was weighed on our side.'

Unfortunately, victory did not bring satisfaction of the Arabs' aspirations, for reasons that have been set down succintly by Air Marshal Sir Robert Saundby,* who took part in many R.A.F. campaigns of the 'twenties: 'With the fall of the Ottoman dynasty at the end of the first World War, large areas of the Middle East had been removed from Turkish rule, and a number of new states were set up. All of them were more or less unorganised, politically unstable, and seriously impoverished, and no oil had yet been found anywhere in the Middle East except in Persia.

'The League of Nations adopted a system whereby certain Great Powers were given mandates to look after one or more of these countries. The Mandatory Power assumed responsibility for the security and development of the new state, and undertook to guide it towards genuine independence. When it was judged that the time was ripe, the Mandatory Power would sponsor the application of the new state for membership of the League of Nations. It would then withdraw its forces and conclude, it was hoped, a treaty of friendship and mutual assistance with its former protegé. The mandates for Iraq (Mesopotamia), Palestine and Transjordan were assigned to the United Kingdom.

'From the very start we encountered many difficulties, which culminated in a serious revolt in Iraq in 1920. There were several reasons for this. The new states were not recognised by Turkey, and were unacceptable to the most powerful Arab ruler of the day, Ibn Saud, the Sheikh of Nejd and later King of Saudi Arabia. As a consequence, there were many border clashes, and a certain amount of infiltration and subversion. The inhabitants had expected too much from the ending of Turkish rule, and were especially disappointed to find that it was still necessary to work for a living. They were inclined to confuse their new-found liberty with a licence to indulge in all sorts of crimes and misdemeanours. Also, they were used to the old system of justice, whereby the party with the

---

* In *The First Air-lift of Troops*, Aircraft Sixty-Nine (Ian Allan Ltd.)

best-filled purse was bound to win, and found our system baffling and unpredictable.

'There was thus a serious threat to both the external and internal security of Iraq. In order to deal with these threats, we had rather more than two divisions of British and Indian combatant troops, four squadrons of the R.A.F., and a considerable amount of what is nowadays called infrastructure. This garrison was tied down to the thankless task of defending hundreds of miles of disputed frontiers against raids and incursions, and in trying to maintain law and order.

'The rebellion put our forces in a position of considerable embarrassment and even danger, and it was suppressed with difficulty. The army appealed for reinforcements, but this caused a great outcry in the press against our whole policy in the Middle East. There was a strong demand to hand back the mandates, bring home our forces, and let the Middle East go its own way. The government was very reluctant to do any such thing, as it knew that our withdrawal would allow the whole area to degenerate into a welter of war. In particular, it feared that without our protection the growing Jewish colony in Palestine, which we had sponsored and encouraged, would be liable to expulsion and even massacre.

'In the hope of finding a solution to this dilemma a conference was convened in Cairo, presided over by Winston Churchill. After the possibility of control by traditional methods had been carefully examined and judged to be impracticable on account of its high cost, Trenchard offered a way out of the deadlock. He proposed that a system of air control should be instituted which, if successful, would cut the cost to a fraction of that needed by the army system. He had to point out, however, that the system was as yet untried, and that its adoption would involve some degree of risk.

'The conference, with some misgivings, decided to accept the risk, and it was agreed that the air force garrison in Iraq should be raised to eight squadrons. All other forces were removed, except for a mixed Brigade of British and Indian infantry, some native levies, and four squadrons of armoured cars manned by the R.A.F. Two squadrons of Vickers Vernon transports (Nos. 45 and 70), two squadrons of D.H.9a's (Nos. 8 and 30), and one fighter squadron equipped with Snipes (No. 1) were stationed at the main airfield at Hinaidi, some six miles south of Baghdad. One squadron of D.H.9a's (No. 84) was at Shaiba, near Basrah, another (No. 55) at Mosul in the north, and one squadron of Bristol Fighters (No. 6) at Kirkuk, in the north-east near the Kurdish border. Most of the troops were stationed at or near Hinaidi.'

The R.A.F. assumed responsibility for the security of Iraq in October 1922, all forces in the country being placed under the command of the A.O.C., Air Vice Marshal Sir John Salmond. It was a bold move as some 33 battalions of infantry, six of cavalry and 16 batteries of artillery had previously been considered necessary for the job; and there was no shortage of prophets predicting the disaster of relying on air control.

It can hardly be said that the aircraft were tailored for the task. Most were of first World War vintage; but this meant, at least, that they were well proven. Their engines were quite reliable by the standards of the day—which was important in an area where a pilot who force-landed sometimes faced, very literally, a fate worse than death. They could land and take off on rough ground, which helped in emergencies, and they were sturdy enough to carry a variety of additional equipment such as goatskins of water, survival rations, and even a spare wheel strapped to the side of the fuselage, in addition to more offensive loads.

The quality of the squadron personnel was high. Salmond himself was to become a Chief of the Air Staff (1930–33). No. 45 Squadron was commanded by Sqn. Ldr. A. T. Harris, remembered today as the great leader of Bomber Command in the second World War. His two flight commanders were Saundby (to be his wartime deputy) and the future Air Chief Marshal Sir Ralph Cochrane.

Harris, typically, was not enamoured of the passive rôle of the Vernon, so he had bomb-racks fitted and cut a hole in the nose of each aircraft, into which a bomb-sight was installed, complete with a remarkable 'Heath-Robinson' bomb-release gear. Their efficiency was recalled by Air Chief Marshal Sir Basil Embry in his autobiography (*Mission Completed*, Methuen). Although serving as second pilot to Saundby, he related: 'When we carried out both training and active bombing, he always used the bombsight and released the bombs while I flew the aeroplane. We worked well together as a team, our average bombing error from 3,000 feet being only ten and a half yards . . . which enabled us to hit the smallest target with all our bombs when we carried out active operations.'

It was not long before the capabilities of the air control force was put to the test. Raids by the Wahabis, from Ibn Saud's territory, were handled without great difficulty, but the situation in the north-east region of Iraq was far more menacing. The Kurds who inhabited the area were not at all happy about being ruled from Baghdad, and when Turkish regular troops began infiltrating into their mountain villages and forts they agreed to help Turkey regain the Mosul area of Iraq in exchange for their independence.

Most influential of their chieftains was Sheikh Mahmud, who had been governor of Sulaimaniya under the Turkish administration. After the war, Britain had appointed him governor of Southern Kurdistan, but dismissed him in 1919 after he had led an armed revolt. Three years later, he was reinstated when it became clear that there was no other practicable way of maintaining a semblance of government authority in the area; but he had lost none of his old rebellious ideas.

So, in February 1923, a considerable force of Kurds and hill Arabs began advancing on Kirkuk, whose garrison could not have coped with the threat unaided. The R.A.F. responded by mounting the first-ever air-lift of troops. Some 480 officers and men of the 14th Sikhs were flown to Kirkuk on board the Vernons of Nos. 45 and 70 Squadrons. When they arrived, part of the town had already been occupied by the rebels, who were terrorising the inhabitants and looting the bazaar, happy in the belief that heavy rains, which had made the roads almost impassable, would prevent reinforcement of the defences. The sight of the Sikhs was enough to make them melt away like magic into the hills, and Kirkuk was saved.

Mahmud was summoned to Baghdad but failed to turn up. So, an ultimatum was dropped to him, reinforced by a number of delayed-action bombs which exploded outside Sulaimaniya at six-hourly intervals. Mahmud resigned and sent a delegation to Kirkuk to parley; but he had no intention of keeping his word and the R.A.F. accordingly attacked his quarters in the town. Mahmud fled to the hills, from where he continued to organise resistance to the British administration.

Two columns of troops were sent to deal once and for all with Mahmud and the Turkish troops who had infiltrated across the border. They were given full support by the R.A.F., which carried out reconnaissance and bombing attacks, ferried rations, stores and clothing to the troops and evacuated the sick and wounded from positions inaccessible to ground transport, two of the Vernons having been specially converted into air ambulances for this duty.

By May 1923, Sulaimaniya had been occupied and Mahmud had sought sanctuary in Persia, with his tribal chiefs. When the British troops withdrew, he returned and declared himself King of Kurdistan. He was informed that this would be tolerated if he left his neighbours in peace. He did so for a while, but the temptation

to raid was too much and he again had to be bombed into retirement on Christmas Day, 1925.

This was not the end of Mahmud, whose periods of relative peace
and 'holy war' against the British continued into the 'thirties.
Fighting was often fierce, as the Kurds were proud and fearless
warriors, rather like the Pathans of India's North-West Frontier.
Often a serious situation was avoided only by the timely arrival of
aircraft—as on May 22nd, 1925, when a flight of Snipes from No. 1
Squadron caught in the open and annihilated a large body of
tribesmen who had threatened to overwhelm a small British detachment. This kind of incident, and the bombing of native villages,
led inevitably to an outcry against 'inhumane' air control methods
by well-intentioned people in Britain and elsewhere. In fact, it is
easy to prove statistically that air control saved lives.

Rebellion and raiding were part of the way of life to Middle
Eastern tribes at that time—almost a sport. Experience had shown
that suppression of such activities by ground forces could be achieved
only at high cost in lives on both sides, for the enemies often included
intense heat and thirst as well as the guns of the opposition.

By comparison, under air control, offenders were instructed to
submit themselves immediately for trial in a court of law. If they
refused, a warning was given, by every possible means, that their
village would be bombed on a certain date. They were recommended
to leave their houses and told that it would not be safe to return
until they were prepared to toe the line.

At the appointed time, the village would be bombed, but it was
quite unnecessary, and even undesirable, to cause any serious
damage. The object was really to institute an air blockade, depriving
the offenders of the shelter and comfort of their homes and to disrupt
their daily routine. Occasionally, however, the house or fort belong-
ing to a particularly recalcitrant leader like Mahmud was selected for
individual destruction, calling for a high degree of bombing accuracy.

After the offenders realised the uselessness of holding out, and
surrendered, troops or police were flown in, with medical staff, to
restore order, treat sickness or wounds, distribute food and generally
rehabilitate the place.

Properly applied, air control never failed, and damage and casualties to both sides were minimal. Its success in Iraq and Transjordan
led to its adoption in the Aden Protectorate. It would have worked
equally well on the North-West Frontier of India, where conditions
were ideally suited to it; but the army retained control there and
R.A.F. squadrons were used only in a support rôle.

Emphasis has been laid in this chapter on operations against Mahmud in Iraq, because that is where the concept of air control was born. It would require a far larger book than this to list all the other actions fought by the R.A.F. in the Middle East in those troubled years, when there were often several skirmishes under way at the same time.

Operations to keep Turkish troops out of Iraq ended in June 1926 with the signing of an agreement by the British, Turkish and Iraqi governments. Eight years of action against Wahabi raiders from the Nejd were brought to a successful conclusion in May 1928, when Ibn Saud gave a written undertaking to restrain his tribes from raiding. In both cases, peace followed countless air actions, supported in the south by armoured car patrols.

In Somaliland, in 1920, twelve D.H.9's collaborated with a small force of the Camel Corps in putting an end to two decades of rebellion by the Mullah. In Egypt, in the same year, an R.A.F. contingent accompanied a punitive expedition sent against the Garjak Nuers in the south-eastern part of Sudan, on the Ethiopian border. Four weeks of bombing and machine-gunning persuaded the native chiefs to sue for peace. Two days' work by No. 14 Squadron were sufficient to cause the surrender of a rebellious sheikh in Transjordan in July 1922. In Aden, the traditional raiding of the fertile northern plateau by Zeidi tribesmen from the Yemen was met with effective counter-attack for the first time in 1925, when twelve Bristol Fighters of the Aden Flight, led by Saundby, gave the Zeidis such a rough time that they were quickly driven back across the border by the local Sultan's 'army', before they had time to reap the crops they had come to collect.

One final operation during this period which must be mentioned, because it was unique and pioneered yet another application of air power in a life-saving rôle, took place in Afghanistan during the Winter of 1928–29.

Inter-tribal disorder in Afghanistan at the end of 1928 and the beginning of 1929 gave the R.A.F. in India, Iraq and the Middle East an opportunity for this unique service. The Shiamwari tribe in Eastern Afghanistan openly rebelled against King Amanullah. They invested Dakka and, taking up a position between Kabul and the Khyber Pass, cut road and telegraph communications. The rebellion spread and the British Legation at Kabul was cut off. On December 14th, 1928, a rebel leader, Kabibullah Khan, advanced on Kabul and established his forces on the Asmai Heights, cutting off the Legation from the rest of the city. The situation became acute, and Sir Francis Humphrys, the British Commissioner, asked that the women and children should be evacuated by air, as shells and bullets were falling on the Legation.

The evacuation of the women and children from the Legation began on December 23rd and ended on February 25th, by which time 586 passengers of various nationalities had been rescued from Kabul.   During these two months the R.A.F. flew 28,160 miles on this duty of evacuation, or 57,438 miles including the journeys from Iraq to Risalpur.   They flew over the mountains, averaging 10,000 ft. in height, during one of the severest winters on record, and over country which offered no opportunity for successful forced landings.

This was a use of military aviation which even its most pacifist critics could not fail to admire and appreciate.

# Chapter Four

# Shoes and Ships and Sealing wax

'*The time has come*', *the Walrus said,*
'*To talk of many things:*
*Of shoes—and ships—and sealing wax—*
*Of cabbages—and kings—*'
*Lewis Carroll: Through the Looking Glass*

IT WOULD BE comparatively easy to run an air force—and, incidentally, to write its history—if one could concentrate on operations to the exclusion of all else. Unfortunately, this is not possible. Napoleon, so it is said, learned from experience that an army marches on its stomach. Trenchard, when he became Chief of the Air Staff, discovered that an air force flies on a vast range of things, at least as varied as the shoes, ships, sealing wax, cabbages and kings with which Lewis Carroll's walrus was concerned.

His broad plan for the future structure of the Royal Air Force was so lucid, far-sighted and comprehensive that even those officers in the Navy and Army who had hoped to carve up and swallow the air forces after the war failed to produce any convincing alternative for discussion; the problems arose when details had to be decided.

Many officers and men of the new service, justly proud of the R.F.C. and R.N.A.S. with which they had served during the long years of war, tried to cling to their old uniforms as long as possible. It was inevitable that they should view with suspicion any replacement for the R.F.C. pilot's 'maternity jacket', which had itself been the subject of criticism when first introduced, or for the smart and traditional navy blue uniform of the R.N.A.S.

In his autobiography, *The Central Blue*, Marshal of the Royal Air Force Sir John Slessor has described vividly his impressions at the unveiling of one early attempt to make members of the R.A.F. distinctive: 'The general atmosphere of drama (was) heightened by gathering dark and the rumble of a practice barrage away on the Westdown ranges. At last, folding doors were thrown back and there, in a very large, rather dark office with the light of a reading lamp upon him, was Mark Kerr in the new R.A.F. uniform, which very few of us had seen before. That first uniform, let's face it, was terrible; a nasty pale blue with a lot of gold all over it, which brought irresistibly to mind a vision of the gentleman who stands outside the cinema.'

Fortunately, this sartorial novelty was soon replaced by the now familiar and universally respected 'R.A.F. blue' uniform.

There was just as much touchiness concerning ranks and titles. The first list, based on established navy and army titles, was quickly shot down. The War Office objected to the fact that naval titles appeared to have been chosen for senior officers and military titles for junior officers. The Admiralty objected to any use of naval titles, even if prefixed by the word 'Air'. So, a list of new and exclusive titles was concocted as follows: Ensign, Lieutenant, Flight-Leader, Squadron-Leader, Reeve, Banneret, Fourth-Ardian, Third-Ardian, Second-Ardian, Ardian and Air Marshal.

Had they been accepted, these strange names would no doubt have become entirely familiar and acceptable with daily usage; but they were not accepted. This may have had something to do with the fact that 'Ardian' suffered by translation, in that it came from the Gaelic 'Ard', meaning chief, and 'Ian' or 'Eun', a bird.

Even the finally-adopted titles met with opposition. The Army objected to the choice of the term 'Marshal' for senior officers, pointing out that only the very highest of their officers, including His Majesty the King, were given the title of Field Marshal, and making great play with the history of the famous Marshals of France. Trenchard's reply was simple and shattering: 'You have given me a number of other people using the term "Marshal" and I am neither affected nor impressed. You have missed out one important person and that is the Provost-Marshal.' Later, in private, he confessed: 'I very nearly said "What about Marshall and Snelgroves?"'

Even so, it took a little time before an ex-R.F.C. Major or ex-R.N.A.S. Lieutenant-Commander learned to accept unselfconsciously the title of Squadron Leader—especially when his squadron comprised an office-full of desks and clerks!

No similar problem existed for the 25,000 women who had been serving as clerical and catering staff, drivers, telephonists, store-keepers and in other capacities in the Women's Royal Air Force at the time of the Armistice. Their contributions had been valuable; their discipline and pride of service were high, confounding the sceptics who predicted all kinds of consequences when girls were drafted to France and Germany in 1919 to replace men eager for demobilisation. But, with the emphasis on economy, they were clearly more expendable than combat units and disbandment of the W.R.A.F. was completed by the end of 1920.

Only in the Royal Air Force Nursing Service (founded in June 1918) did women survive the economy axe. They were established as a permanent branch of the R.A.F. in January 1921 and became Princess Mary's Royal Air Force Nursing Service in June 1923.

Far from being wearied by the seemingly-endless task of creating the first great independent air force in history, Trenchard continued to take a personal interest in every detail, particularly when it had a bearing on 'Air Force spirit'. Tired of continual arguments on the best design for an R.A.F. ensign, he went off one day to see King George V privately. Laying a colour sketch of an ensign before the King, he said: 'During the last war thousands of our young men died for their country under this emblem, the red, white and blue roundel. What better ensign could be given to the R.A.F. than this emblem against a sky-blue background?' All further argument was quashed, as the ensign received immediate Royal assent; but the Secretary of State, Winston Churchill, was very offended because he had not been consulted.

The re-deployment of the post-war R.A.F. went more or less according to plan, although considerable ingenuity was required to meet all the commitments with a decimated force of wartime aircraft that were unlikely to be replaced or supplemented for years.

Of the two home commands, Inland Area was responsible for everything from home defence and strategic attack to balloon training and the R.A.F. section of the Imperial War Museum. Its twin-engined bomber force was not exactly formidable, consisting merely of 'D' Flight of No. 100 Squadron at Spittlegate, equipped with Vimys of the kind used by Alcock and Brown for their pioneer non-stop transatlantic flight. Coastal Area Command, formed in December 1919, controlled all units working with the Navy, including airships under naval control and units afloat in H.M. aircraft carriers.

It is often implied that the sea-going units were treated as a 'Cinderella service' while under R.A.F. control, receiving second-rate equipment bought with what was left of the defence budget when the needs of land-based air power had been met. In some respects, it is difficult to justify such assertions. For example, the first new single-seat fighter ordered in quantity for the R.A.F. after the war was the Fairey Flycatcher, which spent most of its operational life afloat. But there were anomalies, not the least being that aircrew received less pay when sent to sea, although it involved loss of the amenities of shore life and the company of family and friends.

The pioneering tradition of the old R.N.A.S. did not lapse with the formation of the R.A.F. On the contrary, almost all of the basic techniques of modern carrier design and deck flying were worked out during the first post-war decade.

Deck landing facilities installed on H.M.S. *Furious* during the first World War had been primitive. Fore-and-aft arrester wires, a few inches apart, were supported six inches above the deck, which measured 284 ft. long by 70 ft. wide. *Furious's* aircraft had skids instead of wheels and the idea was that the horns on these skids would engage under the wires to bring the aircraft to a halt. If they overran the wires, they were stopped by a rope crash barrier, at considerable cost in broken propellers and buckled wings.

A worse hazard was that the midships funnel and superstructure produced dangerous air currents over the rear deck. So when the war ended, the Navy and R.A.F. engaged in an extensive programme of carrier research with H.M.S. *Argus*.

By then, this ship had been bestowed with the somewhat uncomplimentary nickname of the 'Flat Iron', which is what she looked like, because the air current troubles of the *Furious* had been taken to heart and the *Argus* had been rebuilt with a completely unobstructed flight deck, 550 ft. long by 68 ft. wide. Even the smoke from her funnels was exhausted at the stern.

Pilots found the result much more attractive than did sailors, for one series of 500 landings on that long, flat deck resulted in only 40 crashes, plus minor damage in 90 of the other touch-downs, which was considered remarkably good at the time.

Most of the trouble was caused by the fore-and-aft wires, because once an aircraft had touched down it was anchored firmly to the deck. If it had too much drift or came in one wing low, so that the wires were engaged by the horns on only one skid, its pilot had no hope of taking off for a second attempt.

In an effort to ensure that both skids would engage, the lift which took aircraft from the *Argus's* deck to the hangar beneath was left nine inches below deck level during operations. The aircraft touched down in this 'pit' and were then braked by running up a slight slope with a narrowing gap between wires and deck.

Use of the lift was superseded later by a recessed pit right across the flight deck and when the new carrier *Eagle* entered service she had also a succession of hinged wooden flaps across her deck, supported by the fore-and-aft wires, so that the aircraft were slowed progressively by knocking down the flaps. Unfortunately, this tended also to remove their undercarriages.

Not until H.M.S. *Courageous* and *Glorious* (sister-ships of the *Furious*) entered service was a completely satisfactory solution found. Instead of fore-and-aft wires and a pit, these carriers were equipped with palisades to catch aircraft that would otherwise have drifted off the side of the deck into the sea, plus transverse 'spring-loaded' arrester wires on the rear part of the deck.

Wheels had already replaced skids: now the horns also gave way to a deck-hook, first tried on a Fairey IIIF, and the modern type of arrester gear was born.

In fact, these ships set the pattern for future carriers, for they introduced also the now-familiar 'island' superstructure on the starboard side of their flight decks. Tests with mobile dummy bridge structures on *Argus* had shown that such an island offered a good bridge position, caused no dangerous air currents, and would not get in the way of pilots, who invariably turned to port if they decided to go round again after a baulked landing.

Since then, the basic deck operating techniques have changed only insofar as they have had to be streamlined and speeded up to cater for ever-increasing aircraft performance.

Combat techniques were also improved continuously. The tactic of torpedo-bombing, pioneered successfully during the war, remained a primary form of attack, even at a time when other air forces believed it to have been outmoded by dive-bombing. This persistance was to be richly rewarded in the second World War, when many great actions were fought by British torpedo-aircraft. Dive-bombing was not neglected, however, and Flycatcher squadrons were famous for their tactic of converging bombing, in which three pilots made simultaneous attacks from different directions, beginning with a steep dive from about 2,000 ft. and ending with a raucous pull-out caused, it was said, by noise from the fluttering propeller tips.

No means of improving the efficiency of ship-borne aircraft was overlooked in this period of dual Admiralty/Air Ministry responsibility. Flycatcher units evolved the 'slip flight' technique, in which aircraft took off straight out of the below-deck hangar along the 60 ft. tapered fore-deck and over the bows of the ship—a favourite trick being to perform a slow roll as soon as they were airborne.

The wartime technique of flying reconnaissance aircraft from platforms erected over the gun-turrets of conventional warships was evolved into the vastly superior scheme of carrying seaplanes on powerful catapults.

Like other countries, Britain experimented with submarine-borne aircraft, the submarine *M.2* being fitted with a hangar and catapult for a specially designed Parnall Peto light reconnaissance biplane. However, the small size of the aircraft limited its usefulness, and the idea was abandoned in 1932, after the *M.2* sank with all hands, due it was believed to the hangar doors being left open when she submerged.

A type of military aircraft which disappeared fairly rapidly from the inventory after the first World War was the airship. Its achievements should not be forgotten, as it is estimated that the British Airship Service flew more than two million miles on routine operations, mostly in an anti-submarine rôle. Nor did it need to feel ashamed of its craft by comparison with the more-publicised Zeppelins. Indeed, the official history comments: 'Although at the outbreak of war the British Airship Service was some 12 years behind the German Service, by the end of the war airships of British design were comparable with, if not superior to, any of those employed by the enemy.'

It must be admitted that some of them owed a great deal to lessons learned from shot-down or captured Zeppelins; but there were only five rigid airships in service at the time of the Armistice, as against 98 non-rigid 'blimps'.

Airship crews did everything possible to justify their continued existence. Between July 2nd and 13th, 1919, Major G. H. Scott, with a crew of 31 and one stowaway, completed the first two-way crossing of the North Atlantic in the R.34. Time for the outward journey from East Fortune, Scotland, to New York was 108 hr. 12 min.; the return flight to Pulham in Norfolk took 75 hr. 3 min. Only two other aircraft had crossed the Atlantic earlier and it was to be five years before another succeeded in doing so.

Nevertheless, in 1920 the Air Ministry decided to abandon its proposed plan to lay down one new rigid airship every two years, on the grounds of financial stringency and the proven superiority of the aeroplane. The R.38 was to be completed for sale to America;

surplus existing craft were to be handed over to the Controller General of Civil Aviation for experimental purposes. In January 1921, the further decision was taken to allow the Airship Service of the R.A.F. to lapse; but efforts to sell the airships still in military service met with no success—probably as a result of an accident to R.38, before delivery to America, with the loss of 43 lives.

Continued lobbying by airship enthusiasts persuaded the Government to continue a programme of limited research aimed at the eventual commercial operation of big rigid airships. The R.33 was used for the first stage of the programme, in which future military potential was also explored. In particular, wartime experiments in the use of airships as 'aircraft-carriers' were continued with the successful launching of a D.H. Humming Bird light aircraft from the R.33 in flight on December 4th, 1925, the pilot being Sqn. Ldr. R. A. de Haga Haig.

Second stage of the programme involved the construction of the R.100 and R.101—largest airships ever built in Britain. The former, built by Vickers, flew successfully to Canada and back in August 1930. The government-built R.101 left Cardington on October 4th of the same year in an attempt to fly to India. She got no further than Beauvais in France, where she struck a hill and burst into flames. Of 54 people on board, 47 died, including Lord Thomson, Secretary of State for Air, Air Vice-Marshal Sir W. Sefton Brancker, Director of Civil Aviation, and Major G. H. Scott. Britain's airship programme died with them, as the decision was taken to break up the R.100 and to abandon all further work on such craft.

So, for the first time since the founding of the Air Battalion of the Royal Engineers, Britain's air forces became equipped exclusively with heavier-than-air craft, except for the tethered, unmanned barrage balloons that were to provide such useful protection for cities and other targets for enemy attack in the second World War.

Two of the changes initiated by the wartime enquiries into aircraft supply and by Trenchard's 'White Paper' had, meanwhile, begun to play a major, if little-publicised, part in building his 'foundations for a castle'.

At Farnborough, the Royal Aircraft Factory had not immediately suspended the design of aeroplanes as recommended by the committee of enquiry in May 1916. In fact, one of its most successful types, the S.E.5 fighter, did not fly until December 1916. However, criticism that the factory had harmed private industry by competing in aircraft production was never really true. No aero-engine had ever been built at Farnborough, except experimentally, prior to the date of the enquiry, and the total of 77 aeroplanes built there included 50 manufactured to assist a private company to fulfil a contract. Gradually, however, the swing to pure research had been effected and there is little doubt that Allied victory in the air in the second World War owed much to work conducted at Farnborough in every field of aviation from aerodynamics and metal structures to instruments, radar, weapon-sights, carrier arrester gear, rescue dinghies, photography and jet-engines.

The other important change was in training methods. Up to the time of the 'Fokker Scourge' of 1915–16, R.F.C. pilots had been taught, basically, how to avoid getting into trouble in the air. One of the outstanding 'characters' of British military aviation, Robert Smith-Barry, thought this was all wrong and sent the authorities in England some suggestions on how pilots ought to be trained for combat flying. He asserted that the fundamental mistake was in not using instructors trained specially for the job and recommended the setting up of a school devoted solely to producing the best possible flying instructors.

Smith-Barry was ordered back to England and given the opportunity to try out his ideas at what became known as the School of Special Flying, at Gosport, near Portsmouth. Standardising on dual-control Avro 504's, he reversed the usual procedure by putting the pupil in the back cockpit and the instructor in front. After a time the old method of communication between the two crew-members, by stick-wagging or hand-waving, was superseded by the 'Gosport tube' one-way 'telephone', consisting of a pliable tube with two ear-pieces for the pupil at one end and a funnel-shape mouth-piece at the other. Most important of all, pupils were taught not how to avoid getting into dangers or difficulties, but how to get out of them and, having done so, to go and repeat the process alone.

Those who remember Gosport in those days of 1917 describe it as a kind of lunatic asylum of the air. Unsuspecting persons driving peacefully along the road near the aerodrome were liable to hear a sudden roar behind, then to be overshadowed by the wings of an Avro at nought feet, and to have the aircraft touch down on the road with the tail just clear of the radiator and take off again without stopping.

One of the finest possible tributes to Smith-Barry's genius was a post-war comment by one of his instructors that: 'The gospel he preached was that the aeroplane was a nice-tempered reasonable machine that obeys the simple honest code of rules at all times and in any weather. And by shedding a flood of light on the mysteries of its control he drove away the fear and the real danger that existed for those who were flying aeroplanes in the blackest ignorance even of first principles.'

An even more significant tribute is that the tradition of the School of Special Flying has been carried on since by the Central Flying School which has been, since March 1920, a school for flying instructors. Its training manuals and methods have set the standard for the world, quite apart from the fact that the pilots of more than 50 foreign air forces have been proud to qualify at its courses.

Most of the R.A.F.'s great pilots and leaders have passed through the C.F.S. at some time or another. In so doing, they have usually acquired something of the unorthodox *élan* of Smith-Barry's men, as well as the finest flying training in the world. Throughout the 'twenties, when Avro 504's still equipped the C.F.S. at Upavon, it was not unusual for poor inexperienced pilots from No. 1 F.T.S. at Netheravon to encounter in flight a frightening apparition in the shape of a 504 from Upavon with someone sitting on the wingtip reading a neatly-folded newspaper. The 'someone' was one of Britain's top pilots, best remembered now for his flying in the Schneider Trophy contests!

Whether or not this was precisely what Trenchard meant when he emphasised the vital importance of 'Air Force spirit' is immaterial: it was certainly part of it. What is more, the spirit even imbued some of the politicians of that era—notably Sir Samuel Hoare (later Lord Templewood), Secretary of State for Air from 1922 to 1929.

Work on the permanent buildings for the R.A.F.'s School of Technical Training (Boys) at Halton had been started when he took office, but year after year passed without the Treasury voting any funds for the equally important Cadet College for officers at Cranwell. While training, the future officers had to live in wartime huts, with nothing in their surroundings to foster a fine tradition or to generate permanency for the College.

There was no shortage of critics who maintained that R.A.F. officers could train perfectly well with the Army at Sandhurst or with the Navy at Dartmouth and, with a general election and probable change of government only weeks away, Sir Samuel Hoare decided that Trenchard's whole great dream might fade if something was not done quickly.

He obtained authority in 1929 for obtaining an architect's plan for the College—no more. Having received the plan, he got together with Trenchard and arranged for his wife to lay the foundation stone on April 26th, 1929, before the dissolution of Parliament. On a wet and windy day, the little party proceeded to Cranwell, where Lady Hoare duly laid the stone in a hayfield. It must have seemed a little unreal to those who saw it happening, as not one penny had been voted for any more stones, but the bluff worked. When the new Labour Government came into power, it built the present college which, in its grandeur, would do credit to Sir Christopher Wren himself.

# Chapter
# Five

# Progress through
# Air Power

*Why didst thou leave the trodden paths of men*
*Too soon, and with weak hands though mighty heart*
*Dare the unpastured dragon in his den?*

Percy Bysshe Shelley: *Adonais*

SINCE THE DAYS OF David and Goliath, there have been countless occasions in military history on which a mighty heart has been sufficient to offset the disadvantage of comparatively weak hands. So it was with the Royal Air Force in the first decade of its life. Despite the penny-pinching of politicians who compelled its pilots to fly outdated biplanes of wood, wire and canvas, the R.A.F. set out to show that there was no desert too vast, no mountain too high and no ocean too wide to pass beneath its wings.

The 'dragons' the pilots faced took less tangible forms, being recognised only as unseen forces that could break up an aeroplane in too fast a dive, or hold it back when it should have gone faster, or starve its pilot—and its engine—of air if he climbed too high. Designers and scientists had to find the solutions to such problems but, in the end, only pilots could prove the solutions to be right—at the risk of their lives.

As already related, the British air forces helped to blaze a trail across what was, one day, to become the most important air route in the world—the North Atlantic. But even before the airship R.34 made its epic two-way crossing, R.A.F. pilots were already operating a modest pioneer 'airline' service between Britain and the continent of Europe.

In December 1918, the Air Ministry formed the 86th (Communication) Wing to provide a rapid means of transport to Paris for members of H.M. Government attending the Peace Conference. The service opened in the following month, and by March 1919 the D.H.4's and Handley Pages of No. 1 (Communication) Squadron, based at Kenley, near London, and No. 2 Squadron, based at Buc, near Paris, were operating as a busy private airline. When their task was completed, six months later, they had made a total of 749 flights between London and Paris, with an average flight time of 2½ hours; and had carried 934 passengers, 1,008 bags of mail and 46 despatches.

An air-mail service was also operated by R.A.F. squadrons for the benefit of the Army of Occupation. Initially, the mail travelled by surface routes to Marquise, near Boulogne, from where Handley Page 0/400's of No. 216 Squadron flew non-stop to Cologne, each loaded with 55 bags of mail. D.H.4's, D.H.9's and D.H.9a's of Nos. 18, 55, 57 and 99 Squadrons acted as 'feeders' to the Army Post Offices scattered between the two terminals.

After a time, the French terminal was transferred to Maisoncelle, site of the battle of Agincourt. Unfortunately, the 0/400's loaded weight of more than six tons proved too much for operation from grass airfields and they had to be withdrawn. The whole task now fell on the D.H. squadrons, but the service was actually extended in March 1919 by introducing a cross-Channel air link between Maisoncelle and Hawkinge or Lympne in Kent and recruiting No. 120 Squadron into the force of flying postmen.

The air mail service did much to restore the morale of British soldiers who had survived the last terrible months of trench warfare only to find themselves retained in a beaten Germany, almost cut off from news of home by devastated surface routes. The Christmas mail of 1918 arrived in Cologne in time for delivery to the troops and, despite a hard winter, only 45 of the planned 1,023 flights had failed to get through up to March 1st. Altogether, 7,731 sacks of mail were flown to Cologne during the eight months in which the service operated: of these, 96 per cent were delivered successfully and 70.3 per cent on time—but not without cost. Pilots who had come safely through the dog-fights and bombing raids on the Western Front died in the Channel or in the hills of the Ardennes and Eifel, through which they had tried to thread their way in bad weather.

The mail service ended on August 15th, 1919, after which the organisation and mail traffic were taken over by Sir Samuel Instone, together with some aircraft and flight and ground personnel. From this nucleus grew the Instone Air Line, one of the pioneer commercial companies that merged eventually to form Imperial Airways.

Quite apart from its direct value to war-weary soldiers in Germany, the mail run to Cologne set the pattern for an even more ambitious postal service which opened in 1921. It was clear from the start that if there was ever to be a network of civil air routes linking Britain with its overseas Dominions and Colonies, the key sectors would be those in the Middle East, where the services from England would divide, south to the African continent and east to India, the Far East and Australasia.

As early as February 1919, Lt. Col. A. T. Wilson, Civil Commissioner of Mesopotamia, decided to attempt the flight from Baghdad to Cairo, to save time on his journey to the Peace Conference in Paris. The D.H.4 in which he set out as a passenger encountered both bad weather and mechanical failure, and he completed the trip by rail. He did, however, make the return journey successfully in a D.H.9.

This encouraged the Air Ministry to look into the possibility of supplying Iraq with aeroplanes by air from Egypt as routine, instead of sending them in cases on the long, slow route through the Red Sea and Persian Gulf. It was not possible to do this via the old caravan route between Damascus and the Euphrates, as about half of it was outside the British zone of influence. The only alternative was to map out a route over the southern part of the Syrian Desert which was, literally, trackless and not particularly sandy.

With considerable ingenuity, a convoy of cars was despatched from Amman, escorted by D.H.9a's of No. 47 Squadron and Handley Pages of No. 70 Squadron. Simultaneously, a similar convoy set out from Baghdad, guided by D.H.9a's of No. 30 Squadron. The two parties met roughly half-way across the desert, at El Jid, and the tracks made by their wheels provided a visible and infallible navigation aid for the first few months during which the R.A.F. flew over the new route.

In 1922, the guide-lines were reinforced by ploughing a track along the whole route. Landing grounds were marked out at intervals of approximately 20 miles, by ploughed circles containing a letter or number. Eventually, underground fuel tanks were installed at two of these landing grounds, about 100 miles from each end of the route—with a complex series of locks to foil the less-scrupulous of the Arab car drivers who found the newly marked-out track a very convenient route to follow when journeying from Baghdad to Damascus or Amman.

The Cairo-Baghdad route was opened officially on June 23rd, 1921, and was flown in five stages: Heliopolis-Jerusalem (260 miles), Jerusalem-Amman (65 miles), Amman-Azrak (55 miles),

Azrak-Ramadi (400 miles) and Ramadi-Baghdad (60 miles). Shortly afterwards, it was used for an official air mail service between Egypt and Iraq, enabling British troops in the latter country to receive letters only five days after they were posted in London, compared with the normal 28 days by sea, via Bombay.

First Squadrons to fly the mail run were Nos. 30 and 47, which had helped to mark out the route, and No. 216 which was equipped initially with twin-engined D.H.10's and then with Vimys. When the Vernons of Nos. 45 and 70 Squadrons arrived in Iraq as part of the air control force they replaced the D.H.9a squadrons, but No. 216 continued to share the work with them for a time. Nos. 45 and 70 maintained the service right up to the beginning of 1927 when Imperial Airways took over the job. So important had it become by then that the Cairo-Baghdad route was chosen as the first overseas sector of what became eventually the worldwide Imperial air routes.

Flights of D.H.9a's and Fairey IIID's made pioneering return flights across North Africa, from Cairo to Kano, and down the whole length of the African continent, from Cairo to the Cape, respectively in 1925–26. Such flights became regular training exercises and helped to point a way for airlines to follow.

Other long-distance flights came into the category of 'showing the flag' in the naval tradition. Flying-boats were particularly suitable for this kind of cruising, and some of the flights they made in the 'twenties were quite remarkable by any standards.

On August 12th, 1927, a mixed flight of four 'boats, comprising the Blackburn Iris II, Saunders-Roe Valkyrie and Short Singapore prototypes, and a Supermarine Southampton, started a Baltic cruise of 9,400 miles. On board the Iris, the flagship, was Sir Samuel Hoare, who found the experience so pleasing that the same aircraft was used in 1928 to carry his Under-Secretary, Sir Philip Sassoon, and Air Commodore Arthur Longmore, Director of Equipment, on a two-months' tour of Mediterannean and Indian air stations.

Far more spectacular were the achievements of a special Far East flight of four Southamptons which left Plymouth Harbour in formation on October 17th, 1927, commanded by Group Captain H. M. Cave-Browne-Cave, for the first official visit to service stations, units, and towns in the farthermost parts of the Empire.

In all, these aircraft covered some 28,000 miles in formation, to Singapore, round Australia, back to Singapore, on to Hong Kong, and then back once more to Singapore. Yet the story of their adventures is difficult to tell, for the simple reason that they had no adventures! So far as danger was concerned, the cruise was as prosaic as that of a P. and O. steamer plying between Tilbury and Bombay. They were troubled by barnacles collecting on their hulls in some harbours, by tar oozing from refuelling lighters and fouling their white hulls, and once by a faulty Primus stove. One or two of the crew members had slight attacks of fever, but of real trouble there was none. The Southamptons and their Napier engines behaved perfectly and everything went according to plan. It was this that made the flight so tremendously impressive—the finest piece of organised formation flying the world had ever seen at that time.

In 1929, three Southamptons of No. 203 Squadron flew from Plymouth to Basrah and then made a further trip of 2,000 miles to Muscat and back. Two Southamptons of the Felixstowe Flying Boat Development Flight cruised to Norway and back. In 1930 four more aircraft of the same type, from Calshot, made a Baltic cruise. Next year a Singapore II and the new Saunders-Roe A.7 flew 6,530 miles to the Middle East and back to Felixstowe.

Each of these, and later flights, made an invaluable contribution to the R.A.F.'s versatility and operational experience. During many of them, the crews lived on board, provision being made for canvas berths, cooking apparatus, and officers' and crews' wardrooms, recalling the motto of Noel Pemberton-Billing, founder of the Supermarine Company, that his flying-boats would be: 'Not aeroplanes which float, but boats which fly.'

These flying-boat cruises helped to demonstrate the growing efficiency and reliability of British aircraft, leading to export orders from many parts of the world. The R.A.F., through the Aeroplane and Armament Experimental Establishment at Martlesham Heath, also contributed immensely to the development of new aircraft in this period when the vintage types left over from the first World War were at last being replaced by newer designs.

All prototypes went to Martlesham for test, and this called for skilled, and often courageous, flying from the service pilots who undertook much of the work. For example, from 1924, new R.A.F. fighters were expected to be able to survive test dives at the maximum speed of which they were capable. The first aircraft to prove its ability to do this was the Gloster Grebe single-seat fighter, which attained 240 m.p.h. before pull-out; but further testing revealed that it had a tendency to wing flutter and Vee bracing struts were eventually added to the top wing extensions. It was, perhaps, as well that, from 1925, wearing of parachutes by R.A.F. aircrews became compulsory.

Having at last received some new aeroplanes, squadrons lost no time in demonstrating their potential to the public who paid for them. Since 1920, the Royal Air Force had staged an annual air display at Hendon Aerodrome, with three main objectives: to familiarise the public with aviation progress, to form part of the annual training of the Service and to provide financial support for R.A.F. charities.

The Hendon Display quickly became a highlight of the aviation year. The first of them attracted over 60,000 people and attendances grew year by year, encouraged by press and newsreel reports of the thrills to be seen there. To his credit, King George V, the 'sailor King' who could never overcome his intense dislike of noisy aeroplanes flown by apparently reckless officers, attended the Hendon Displays regularly. In 1925, when No. 25 Squadron put on a particularly memorable display of formation aerobatics in its Grebes, he directed operations at one stage by radio-telephony—a very new departure at that time.

The question of who originated formation aerobatics never fails to provoke heated arguments, but there is little doubt that the Royal Air Force has, from the earliest times right up to the present day, set the standard for others to follow. As early as 1921, an account of the R.A.F. Display in the *Royal Air Force Record* told how: 'five C.F.S. Snipes did the most wonderful formation flying that ever happened. This was, as last year, undoubtedly the best show of the lot and was worth going miles to see. They looped, they rolled, they dived, all in wonderful formation; not content with that, they did much upside down flying, in line and in V formation, still with their distances exact.'

By 1933, R.A.F. formation aerobatics had advanced to the stage where nine Hawker Furies of No. 25 Squadron could take off tied together with light rubber cables and perform a loop, still linked in Vee formation, over the centre of the aerodrome before breaking up into flights for even more spirited manoeuvres. The weather on the day of the Display that year was atrocious, yet the aircrews went through almost the entire scheduled programme.

Audax army co-operation aircraft demonstrated the techniques of supply dropping and picking up with a hook messages in a bag suspended on a line between two posts—as practised by air control squadrons overseas. Bulldog fighters made mock attacks on a Sidestrand twin-engined bomber. A succession of fighter squadrons performed faultless aerobatics. Two instructors from No. 2 F.T.S. put on the traditional display of 'pupil and instructor' crazy flying

in 504's. Bulldogs fired dummy ammunition at a target sleeve
towed by a Fairey Gordon. Flying-boats and amphibians flew past
with stately decorum. C.F.S. instructors performed in their new
Tutor trainers, which were beginning to supersede the veteran 504,
the leader causing something of a sensation by performing an
upward bunt, starting from an inverted position at low altitude.

There was much more before the show ended with an attack by
a 'Blueland' force on 'Redland's' coastal base, complete with chem-
ical factory, docks, a lighthouse, a pier and a seaplane of curious
design, all defended by anti-aircraft guns, a fighter squadron and
an observation balloon. The balloon was shot down, its occupant
'Wing Cdr. Sandbags' escaping by parachute. The base went up
in a satisfactory show of pyrotechnics. Opposing fighter squadrons
engaged in a dogfight with great gusto. Finally, the seaplane, too,
went up in a great shower of water, matching that which had come
downward all day.

Thus, the show was far from being a wash-out and *The Aeroplane*
commented: 'Only a force, part of whose daily work is to keep
accurate formation, to find their target with bomb and machine-gun,
to snatch a message from a string, to loop and roll and dive with
beautiful precision, and to pursue and fight the enemy in the air,
could have done these things under the deplorable conditions of
this year's display.'

The aircraft of 1933 were, except for the 504's, mostly of second-
or third-generation post-war vintage. Construction had changed
from wood to metal, although airframes were still fabric-covered.
Supercharging of the engines had raised the service ceiling of the
fighters from 20,000 ft. in 1919 to 28,000 ft. in the case of the Fury
—an important quality, as the first World War had proved that
victory in air combat often went to the pilot who could dive on
his opponent from above, 'out of the sun'.

Even more significant was that the Fury reflected a growing
preference for clean, liquid-cooled in-line engines rather than the
big, bluff air-cooled radials that had powered most fighters designed
in the 'twenties. Radials avoided the need for a heavy, vulnerable
water cooling system, but produced considerable drag, even after
the invention of, first, the Townend ring and, later, NACA-type
cowlings.

The great British protagonist of the in-line engine was Sir Richard
Fairey. During a visit to America in 1923, he was so impressed by
the cleanly-cowled 480 hp. Curtiss D.12 engines he saw there that
he acquired licence rights and fitted British-built D.12 (Fairey

Felix) engines in new bomber and fighter prototypes which he named the Fox and Firefly respectively. Trenchard personally ordered a squadron of Foxes, which advanced the speed of R.A.F. day-bombers by 50 m.p.h., enabling them to outfly any fighter in service.

The performance of these Fairey types, with their 'eversharp' noses, did not escape the notice of other designers, and the adoption of Rolls-Royce liquid-cooled in-line engines for many subsequent combat types contributed immensely to R.A.F. superiority in the air in the 1930's and 40's.

One of the first designers to follow Fairey's example was the great Sydney Camm, who led the Hawker design team for an unmatched period of over 40 years from 1925 onward. The world-beating association of Hawker airframes and Rolls-Royce engines began with the Hart bomber and Fury fighter of the late 'twenties, the latter being the first R.A.F. fighter in squadron service to exceed 200 m.p.h.

So fine were these aircraft, and the infinite variety of derivatives such as the Audax, Hind, Hardy, Demon, Hector and Naval Osprey and Nimrod, that by the mid-thirties there were more Hawker aeroplanes in the R.A.F. than all other types combined.

They descended in force—rank after rank—on Mildenhall Aerodrome, in Suffolk, for the Review of the Royal Air Force that was part of the celebrations to mark the Silver Jubilee of King George V's reign in 1935. But, although the assembled squadrons made an impressive sight numerically, almost all the aircraft were biplanes. Several front-line bomber squadrons were even equipped still with big lumbering Vickers Virginias, dating from the early 'twenties and with a top speed of 108 m.p.h. The fighters still carried the standard 1918 armament of two synchronised Vickers machine-guns.

There was no suggestion that British designers had lost their ability to produce aircraft as advanced as any in the world. It happened simply to be another of Britain's periodic times of financial 'squeeze', when defence is the traditional target for the most crippling cuts in expenditure.

Proof of industry's capability had been given by a series of superb world records set up by British aircraft with R.A.F. pilots.

Piloted by Sqn. Ldr. Gayford and with Flt. Lt. G. E. Nicholetts as navigator, a Fairey Long-range Monoplane had flown non-stop from Cranwell to Walvis Bay in South West Africa on February 6–8th, 1933, raising the World Distance Record to 5,309 miles. But it was the achievements of the R.A.F.'s High Speed Flight in the Schneider Trophy contests that had really captured the imagination of the public.

When it was presented by Jacques Schneider in 1913, this famous Trophy was intended to encourage steady improvement in the design of seaplanes and flying-boats. British civilian pilots won the 1914 and 1922 contests; but by the mid-twenties victory in the Schneider contests carried so much prestige for the winning nation that several countries began developing specially-designed racing seaplanes, with government funds, against which private entries stood little chance of success.

Realising that experience gained in building such aircraft would lead to future improvements in its combat equipment, the Air Ministry not only ordered a series of high-speed seaplanes to compete in the 1927 contest at Venice but agreed to provide pilots for them.

The contest was won by Flt. Lt. S. N. Webster in a Supermarine S.5 monoplane with an 875 h.p. Napier Lion engine, at a speed of 281.65 m.p.h. In doing so, he set up a new international speed record of 283.66 m.p.h. over a 100-km. circuit. In the following year, Flt. Lt. D'Arcy Greig raised the British national speed record to 319.57 m.p.h. in an S.5.

For the next contest, in 1929, Supermarine's chief designer, R. J. Mitchell, produced the S.6, with very similar lines but powered by a Rolls-Royce 'R' twelve-cylinder racing engine developing a fantastic 1,900 h.p. The contest was won by Flying Officer H. R. D. Waghorn, at a speed of 328.63 m.p.h. In a similar aircraft, Flying Officer R. L. R. Atcherley set up new international records of 332 and 331 m.p.h. around 50 and 100-km. circuits respectively. On September 12th, 1929, Sqn. Ldr. A. H. Orlebar raised the World's absolute speed record to 357.7 m.p.h.

Despite the drag of their big floats, Mitchell's seaplanes had proved themselves faster than any landplane ever built and in 1931 he provided the High Speed Flight with an aircraft that not only won the Schneider Trophy outright for Britain, with a third consecutive victory, but put the speed record above 400 m.p.h. for the first time.

This aircraft, the S.6B, differed little from the S.6 as the Air Ministry could not afford to subsidise design of a new aircraft. In fact, Britain would not have been able to compete at all but for the generosity of Lady Houston who agreed to finance the entry if the R.A.F. would provide the pilots. The winner was Flt. Lt. J. N. Boothman, at a speed of 340.6 m.p.h. Later the same month, on September 29th, Flt. Lt. G. H. Stainforth showed the full capability of the S.6B and its Rolls-Royce engine—now boosted to 2,600 h.p. —by raising the world speed record to 407.5 m.p.h.

Mitchell felt sure that he could produce a fighter aircraft of unbeatable performance, based on experience gained with the Schneider racers. Camm had similar ideas. Rolls-Royce had the ability to build engines for the kind of aircraft they were planning. At the Air Ministry, a young officer named Ralph Sorley was working on revolutionary new armament concepts that would give such fighters unprecedented fire-power. It needed only a political decision to translate paper projects into ironmongery that would make the R.A.F. the best-equipped air force in the world. That decision could be delayed no longer when the government learned of the great new air force that was being created in secret by Adolf Hitler, the German dictator, in defiance of the Versailles Peace Treaty.

# Chapter Six

# A Castle at Last

*In peace there's nothing so becomes a man*
*As modest stillness and humility:*
*But when the blast of war blows in our ears,*
*Then imitate the action of the tiger;*
*Stiffen the sinews, summon up the blood,*
*Disguise fair nature with hard-favour'd rage;*
*Then lend the eye a terrible aspect.*

*William Shakespeare: King Henry V*

THE TIME HAD come to build a castle instead of a cottage on the foundations laid by Trenchard in 1919; would they stand the test? Could the British aircraft industry, accustomed to building biplanes at leisurely pace, gear itself quickly enough to produce entirely new types of aircraft in huge quantities? Could the almost inevitable war with Hitler's Germany be deferred long enough for the new aircraft to become operational? If the answer to these, or any one of a dozen other questions, had been negative, Volume Two of this history would have been very brief and Volume Three non-existent.

It was not sufficient to modernise the equipment of the Royal Air Force; its whole structure had to be changed to meet the new situation. There had already been some changes, the first of them dating back to 1923, when Sir Samuel Hoare had become Secretary of State for Air. On taking office, he discovered that the strength of the R.A.F. had increased by only two squadrons since 1920, to a total of 35 at home and overseas.

It seemed that the effectiveness of strategic bombing, proved in the first World War by the Independent Force, was being ignored completely by those responsible for the defence of the United

Kingdom, which was wide open to a form of attack far more sudden and easy to carry out than conventional invasion by sea. So a committee was set up under the chairmanship of the Marquess of Salisbury to study the whole question of national and imperial defence, with particular emphasis on (i) the relations of the Navy and R.A.F. as regards the control of fleet air work, (ii) the corresponding relation between the Army and the R.A.F., and (iii) the standard to be aimed at for defining the strength of the air force for purposes of home and imperial defence.

The R.A.F. was well enough established by 1923 not to fear that items (i) and (ii) would lead to its division among the older services. However, the Navy and Army were given complete operational control of R.A.F. detachments working with them, the Navy having in addition full disciplinary control on board ship. Design and provision of aircraft and initial training remained the responsibility of the R.A.F., with the proviso that the Army and Navy should be consulted at every stage to ensure that their requirements would be met as fully as possible. An important aid to closer collaboration between the services was the decision to attach or second Army and Naval officers to the R.A.F.

The Navy undertook to provide the bulk of the pilots for carrierborne R.A.F. units by the attachment of naval officers to the Air Force. From that time, too, air spotting and reconnaissance duties were performed exclusively by naval aircrew not attached to the R.A.F. These changes led in April 1924 to the establishment of the Fleet Air Arm, embodying those units of the R.A.F. normally embarked in carriers and fighting ships.

Initially, the F.A.A. was organised on a flight basis, with approximately six aircraft per flight; but in 1933 units embarked in carriers reverted from flights to squadrons (nine to twelve aeroplanes) numbered from 800 upward. The original flight basis of six aircraft was retained for units providing aircraft for battleships and cruisers, the strength of the complete force so becoming 12 squadrons and six flights. This organisation was maintained until 1937, when control of the Fleet Air Arm passed to the Admiralty.

So far as the main air defence policy was concerned, the Salisbury Committee issued an interim report which formed the basis of a statement by the Prime Minister, Stanley Baldwin, in Parliament on June 20th, 1923. This laid down that: 'In addition to meeting the essential air power requirements of the Navy, Army, Indian and Overseas Commitments, British air power must include a Home Defence Air Force of sufficient strength adequately to protect us against air attack by the strongest air force within striking distance of this country . . . In the first instance the Home Defence Force should consist of 52 squadrons, to be created with as little delay as possible, and the Secretary of State for Air has been instructed forthwith to take preliminary steps for carrying this decision into effect. The result of this proposal will be to add 34 squadrons to the authorised strength of the Royal Air Force. The details of the organisation will be arranged with a view to the possibility of subsequent expansion.'

This was the programme that remained the basis of R.A.F. policy for a full decade, until the advent of Hitler's *Luftwaffe* necessitated still greater expansion.

The new Air Defence of Great Britain (A.D.G.B.) Command came into being as a unified force in 1925, Air Marshal Sir John Salmond being appointed as its first Air Officer Commanding-in-Chief on his return from Iraq. The build-up to full strength was expected to take five years, with a solid foundation of *élite* regular squadrons supported by units based upon the great centres of industry, on the lines of the Territorial Army.

Creation of the non-regular force began at once, the intention being that, of the total of 52 squadrons (35 bomber, 17 fighter), six should be Auxiliary Air Force squadrons, raised and maintained by County Associations, and seven others should be Special Reserve squadrons.

In mid-1926, the A.D.G.B. was organised as the Wessex Bombing Area (regular bomber squadrons), and a Fighting Area (fighter squadrons). These were supplemented in due course by No. 1 Air Defence Group, embodying the A.A.F. and Special Reserve squadrons. Under a further reorganisation in 1933, the units which had been under the Wessex Bombing Area and No. 1 Air Defence Group were redistributed amongst the Western Area (with headquarters at Andover), the Central Area (Abingdon) and No. 1 Air Defence Group (Auxiliary Squadrons). The Wessex Bombing Area was discontinued; the Fighting Area remained as before.

The other home commands also remained largely unchanged, with Inland Area controlling five squadrons of Audax army co-operation aircraft in 1933 and Coastal Area controlling one bomber and four flying-boat squadrons, as well as administrating the R.A.F. units in the Fleet Air Arm.

Overseas Commands included the R.A.F. Middle East (headquarters in Cairo) with three bomber squadrons, one army co-operation squadron and one bomber-transport squadron; Transjordan and Palestine Command (Jerusalem), with two bomber squadrons and an armoured car company; British Forces in Iraq (Hinaidi) with three bomber squadrons, one bomber-transport squadron, one flying-boat squadron and an armoured car company; R.A.F. India (New Delhi), with four bomber squadrons, four army co-operation squadrons and a bomber-transport flight; R.A.F. Mediterranean (Malta), with one flying-boat squadron; Aden Command, with one bomber squadron and an armoured car section; and Royal Air Force, Far East (Singapore), with one bomber squadron, one torpedo-bomber squadron and one flying-boat squadron.

Numerically, as already stated, this was quite an air force. When therefore, the Foreign Secretary, Sir John Simon, and Anthony Eden went to Berlin in March 1935 to discuss an air pact with Hitler, they had every reason to be shaken by his claim that the *Luftwaffe* was already as strong as the R.A.F. and that his objective was parity with France. As the R.A.F. then had at least 3,000 operational aircraft, including reserves, the Air Staff suggested that Hitler was mistakenly comparing Britain's first-line strength with the *Luftwaffe's* total strength; but the Cabinet preferred to believe Hitler. In the event it is as well that they did so, for otherwise they might not have agreed to such a vast—and entirely essential—expansion of the R.A.F.

As Hitler had boasted that his air force would equal that of France by 1937, and the French were estimated to have 1,500 first-line aircraft, the initial target was to build up the R.A.F. to a total of 1,512 first-line aircraft in 123 squadrons at home by March of that year. But Germany was not the only potential enemy. In October 1935, Italian forces invaded Ethiopia and Mussolini's 'Eagles' were soon gaining glory by dropping high-explosive and mustard gas bombs on poorly-armed tribesmen. Several additional squadrons of R.A.F. combat aircraft were despatched to the Middle East, but no direct action was taken in support of the Ethiopians and Mussolini added a vast territory to his empire with little more effort that Hitler had expended in re-occupying the Rhineland.

With Japan becoming even more belligerent in the Far East, the government soon had qualms about the adequacy of the expansion scheme. In February 1936, the target for the R.A.F. at home was raised to 1,736 first-line aircraft, in 124 squadrons, by March 1939, plus ten more squadrons each for the overseas air forces and Fleet Air Arm. Nor was that all. Strike power was to be increased enormously by replacing light bombers with medium bombers, and much larger reserves were to be created, until they totalled 225 per cent of the first-line strength. To meet these new demands, a 'shadow factory' scheme was inaugurated, under which the nation's leading motor car manufacturers were to set up huge assembly plants for aircraft and aero-engines to supplement the steadily-growing output from the aviation industry.

To man the additional aircraft, the Auxiliary Air Force undertook to form more squadrons. It was also lumbered, somewhat against its will, with the task of creating a large number of balloon barrage squadrons to protect London. However, it could not possibly grow sufficiently to provide all the urgently-needed manpower; so, in April 1937, a new organisation known as the Royal Air Force Volunteer Reserve began to take in men for training as pilots of non-commissioned rank. Drawing its recruits from hitherto-un-tapped sources in industrial areas and from grammar schools, the R.A.F.V.R. was intended to produce 800 pilots a year: in fact, it had 5,000 pilots either fully-trained or under training by September 1939.

By then, the V.R. had been extended to cover the complete range of aircrew, medical, equipment, administrative and technical branches. There were also nearly 8,000 officers and airwomen in the Women's Auxiliary Air Force, formed in June 1939 out of former companies of the Auxiliary Territorial Service working with the R.A.F.

Even civilians of both sexes, and assorted ages and backgrounds, rushed to form a last-ditch reserve of pilots by joining the Civil Air Guard in the Summer of 1938. The incentive was an opportunity of learning to fly with the aero clubs at a cost of from half-a-crown to ten shillings an hour. The commitment was an undertaking to accept service in any capacity or rank in connection with aviation in this country in the event of emergency arising from war or threat of war.

The threat grew as year succeeded year. When civil war broke out in Spain in 1936, Hitler and Mussolini took advantage of the opportunity to test squadrons of their latest combat aircraft in action, in support of General Franco's insurgents. The high quality of *Luftwaffe* fighters and bombers was soon demonstrated, as was the devastation that could be caused by ruthless air attacks on poorly defended cities.

Hitler no longer attempted to disguise his ambition. On March 12th, 1938 he annexed Austria to his Third Reich which, he predicted, would last a thousand years. Next on the list was Czechoslovakia, which was to be smashed by military action not later than October 1st, 1938. On the initiative of the British Prime Minister, Neville Chamberlain, Mussolini called a summit meeting of the heads of state of Germany, Italy, Britain and France. The agreement they signed at Munich, without consulting the Czechs, ceded to Germany all areas of Bohemia and Moravia which had had a German-speaking population of 50 per cent or more in 1910.

Whatever one's feeling might be in retrospect concerning this shameful agreement, it is impossible to doubt the sincerity of Neville Chamberlain, who firmly believed that its signature had secured 'peace in our time'. In fact, the rest of Czechoslovakia was gobbled up by Hitler within six months, virtually without a struggle, and the dictator who professed publicly 'no more territorial ambitions in Europe' began to plan how he would seize the Polish Corridor separating East Prussia from the remainder of Germany.

The real, if unintentional, benefit gained from the Munich agreement was that it gave the Royal Air Force one more year in which to prepare for war. That year saw not only an increase in the number of front-line aircraft but, more importantly, an immeasurable improvement in fighting efficiency because of the replacement of veteran biplane bombers and fighters by modern monoplanes.

The best R.A.F. fighter of 1935 had been the Gloster Gauntlet biplane, armed with two machine-guns and with a top speed of 230 m.p.h. By 1939, both the Hawker Hurricane and Supermarine Spitfire fighters were operational, each armed with eight machine-guns (arranged to fire outside the propeller disc and, therefore, requiring no synchronisation gear) and with maximum speeds of 316 m.p.h. and 355 m.p.h. respectively. If war had come in September 1938, there would have been only 93 Hurricanes and Spitfires, plus 573 obsolescent biplanes, to oppose about 1,200 modern German bombers. Twelve months later, there were more than 500 of the eight-gun monoplane fighters in service.

Equal progress was made with the bomber force in the four years of the pre-war expansion programme. Best heavy bomber of 1935 had been the Handley Page Heyford with an armament of three guns, bomb load of 1,600 lb. for a 920-mile range and maximum speed of 142 m.p.h. By comparison, the Vickers Wellington of 1939 carried six guns and 4,500 lb. of bombs over a 1,200-mile range and could fly at 235 m.p.h.

Lessons learned in the Schneider Trophy contests had been well applied. The Spitfire inherited the fine lines of Mitchell's S.6B; while the Rolls-Royce Merlin engine installed in both the Spitfire and Hurricane owed much to the 'R' engine developed for the

Schneider Trophy seaplanes. In both fighters, monoplane layout was combined with a retractable undercarriage, enclosed cockpit and many other technical refinements. The bombers, too, were thoroughly up-to-date. In particular, their defensive armament consisted usually of powered multi-gun turrets, combining high fire-power with protection for the gunners.

As well as re-equipping, the R.A.F. had reorganised for war. In July 1936, the Air Defence of Great Britain Command ceased to exist and the home force was divided into four new Commands, each with a specific rôle. Bomber Command took over control of all bomber squadrons. Fighter Command became responsible for fighter and army co-operation squadrons and the Observer Corps, a large body of civilian volunteers trained to plot and report with great precision every aircraft flying over and around the U.K. Coastal Command was allocated all flying-boat and general reconnaissance squadrons, plus certain training units, and was also made responsible for the administration and shore training of Fleet Air Arm squadrons. Training Command assumed responsibility, with few exceptions, for all training units in the U.K.

Although Trenchard had retired in 1929, to be succeeded first by Air Chief Marshal Sir John Salmond, he must have rejoiced to see the comparative smoothness with which the new and very large Royal Air Force of the late 'thirties was built up on the small but sound nucleus he had created so many years earlier. But even he may not have known much about the invisible eyes of radar that were beginning to peer from our coasts to enhance beyond measure the efficiency of Fighter Command, or the revolutionary aero-engines without propellers that were being developed by a young R.A.F. officer named Frank Whittle, or the mighty four-engined bombers that were taking shape to Air Ministry specifications issued in 1936.

Something else that neither he nor anyone else in Britain could know for certain was that the *Luftwaffe*, too, had grown in five years from a motley collection of 400 aircraft and 20,000 men to a well-trained force of 3,609 modern combat aircraft, 552 transport aircraft and over half a million men. Only in retrospect can we see that when war finally came, on September 3rd, 1939, the Royal Air Force was superior to the *Luftwaffe* in everything but numbers, and that Britain's aircraft designers and scientists were capable of offsetting even that one deficiency.

The Royal Air Force came into being on April 1, 1918. Before that, military flying in Britain had been pioneered by the Royal Engineers and then developed by the Royal Flying Corps and Royal Naval Air Service before and during the 1914–18 War. The first 25 pages of illustrations in this volume pay tribute to the achievements of these predecessors of the R.A.F.

A balloon being packed by the Balloon Section of the Royal Engineers on Laffan's Plain, Farnborough, about 1894. Four balloon sections played an active part in the Boer War which began in 1899, their main role being to spot targets for the artillery. [*I.W.M.*

'Col'. S. F. Cody supervising the ascent of one of his man-lifting kites at Farnborough. In 1906 Cody was appointed Chief Instructor in 'kiting' to the Balloon School, which had formed a man-lifting kite section in June 1894, after experiments by Capt. B. F. S. Baden Powell had shown that kites might be more easily transportable and less vulnerable than observation balloons. The man-lifting kites were attached to a cable, which was suspended in the air by a number of 'lifter 'kites, the topmost kite being about 1,000 feet up.

First of the airships to be built at Farnborough was *Nulli Secundus* of 1907;
here the 'ship is in its modified form, a year later, over Farnborough camp.

The distinction of being 'British Army Aeroplane No. 1' went to this 52ft-span
two-seat pusher biplane powered by a 50 h.p. Antoinette engine—actually the
one which had powered the airship *Nulli Secundus*. Construction of the machine
began late in 1907 under conditions of strict secrecy and the first real flight,
as opposed to a short hop, was made on October 16, 1908, on Farnborough
Common.  This was the first recognised powered and sustained flight in
Great Britain.  Photo shows the machine as it appeared after the removal of
its biplane tail and the installation of mid-gap ailerons.

A Bristol Boxkite biplane being prepared for a flight during Army manoeuvres on Salisbury Plain in September 1910. This aircraft was flown by Capt. Bertram Dickson whilst another Boxkite was flown in the manoeuvres by Lt. Robert Loraine. Incidentally, the occasion marked the first use in this country (though just ante-dated by J. R. D. McCurdy in America) of air-to-ground radio communication, using a spark and coherer apparatus.

When, in December 1910, a crashed Army Blériot monoplane, known as the 'Man-killer', was sent from Larkhill to the Balloon Factory, Farnborough, for repair, Mervyn O'Gorman asked the Master General of Ordnance if his authorisation could cover reconstruction of the machine. This was agreed and eventually the tractor monoplane was changed into a tail-first biplane—the S.E.1 (see photo), only aircraft built in the original S.E. (Santos Experimental) category.

Unfortunately it inherited its forbear's unpleasant characteristics and crashed in August 1911, killing its pilot.

Shortly after the 'Factory' had embarked upon the rebuilding of the Blériot 'man-killer' early in 1911, it was given another opportunity to put its own design ideas into practical form when a Voisin pusher biplane owned by the War Office arrived for repair. By subterfuge it was 'reconstructed' with the result shown in the photograph—the B.E.1, dubbed the 'Silent Army Aeroplane' because its 60 h.p. Renault vee-eight engine was so quiet in comparison with the contemporary rotary engines. The B.E.1 performed valuable service for three years and was used, among other things, for experiments in wireless transmission.

In January 1912, Lt. C. R. Samson, first R.N.A.S. pilot to qualify, flew the Short S.38 pusher from staging erected over the foredeck of H.M.S. *Africa*, riding at anchor at Sheerness, thus imitating for the first time in Europe a similar feat performed some months earlier by Eugene Ely in the United States. In May 1912 during the Royal Naval Review at Weymouth, Samson flew off a staging on H.M.S. *Hibernia* while steaming at 15 knots. Pictures show H.M.S. *Hibernia* with Short S.38 on special staging and (*right*) the S.38 rising from the ship.

One of the most far-sighted moves in 1912 was the setting up of a Central Flying School at Upavon on Salisbury Plain, where pilots of both R.F.C. Wings could be trained to a common high standard. This photograph shows some of the School's B.E.2a and Maurice Farman trainers lined up in front of the wooden hangars in 1913.                    [*Flight International*

A Henri Farman F.22 two-seater, armed with a forward-firing Vickers gun, flying at Farnborough on June 11, 1913.                    [*I.W.M.*

Early seaplane handling. Short improved S.41 seaplane being beached at the
R.N.A.S. station at Yarmouth during the naval manoeuvres in the summer of 1913.

Aerial view of the 'Concentration Camp' at Netheravon, June 29, 1914, when war was but a few weeks away. The aircraft include B.E.2s, the high-altitude R.E.5, Maurice Farman Shorthorns, Blériot monoplanes, Avro 500s and Henri Farmans. Note the 'T' hangars, one of which is seen collapsed in the foreground.

A B.E.2a approaches as General Sir Horace Smith-Dorrien takes the salute at the first air review in May 1913 on Perham Down. The B.E.2a was developed at the Royal Aircraft Factory by F. M. Green and Geoffrey (later Sir Geoffrey) de Havilland in 1912 and was powered by a 70 h.p. Renault engine which gave it a maximum speed of 65-70 m.p.h.

Henri Farman biplanes of the R.F.C. on Farnborough Common in 1915, or earlier.

First R.F.C. aircraft to land in France during the 1914-18 War was B.E.2a No. 347 of No. 2 Squadron, which left Dover at 6.25 a.m. on August 13, 1914, piloted by Lt. H. D. Harvey-Kelly, and landed near Amiens at 8.20 a.m.— almost 2 hours later. This photograph was taken at Lythe, near Whitby (Yorkshire) and Lt. Harvey-Kelly is seen on the right, studying a map. He was killed in action behind the German lines on April 29, 1917.          [I.W.M.

The R.F.C.'s first reconnaissance flight of the 1914-18 War, on Wednesday, August 19, 1914. Participants were Captain Joubert de la Ferté of No. 3 Squadron, flying a Blériot XIbis monoplane, and Lt. G. W. Mapplebeck of No. 4 Squadron in a B.E.2b. (From a painting by K. McDonough.)

[*Flight International*

One of the few types to complete all the 1912 Military Aeroplane Trials successfully was the Blériot XI monoplane, examples of which served with the R.F.C. and R.N.A.S. as reconnaissance and training machines early in the 1914-18 War. Here is a parasol-winged version used by the R.F.C., sporting the Union Jack, the original national marking of the U.K., and (below) wearing what eventually became the standard markings—the roundel and the rudder stripes in red, white and blue, with blue leading.

Pioneer naval aviator C. R. Samson—distinguished, among other things, for his work with the armoured cars in Belgium—standing in front of two Nieuport X scouts on No. 3 (R.N.A.S.) Squadron's airfield at Tenedos during the Gallipoli campaign late in 1914. Note the Nieuport's single Lewis gun mounted to fire upwards through the centre-section of the top wing.    [*I.W.M.*

Starting for Friedrichshafen. These three Avro 504s standing on the airfield at Belfort in November 1914 are the actual machines in which Sqn. Cdr. E. F. Briggs (Avro No. 873), Flt. Cdr. J. T. Babington (No. 875) and Flt. Lt. S. V. Sippe (No. 874) carried out their historic bombing raid on the Zeppelin works and sheds at Friedrichshafen on November 21, 1914. Briggs was brought down by ground fire but his comrades returned safely to base. Another Avro which was scheduled for the mission was forced to retire owing to a broken tailskid. Incidentally, these Avros were reputedly the first bombers in the world to be fitted with mechanical bomb releases.

Delivery by hand.  An R.N.A.S. pilot dropping a bomb over the side of the cockpit of an airship control car.  In the early days of the war bombs were dropped from aeroplanes in this manner.          [ *I.W.M.*

Vickers F.B.5. Popularly known as the 'Gun Bus', this two-seat fighter, armed with a movable Lewis gun in the front cockpit (the gun is not shown in our picture), began to reach the Western Front early in 1915. In 1916 it shared with the F.E.2b and the D.H.2 in overcoming the superiority of the Fokker Eindekker E.1 single-seat fighter. The F.B.5 was not finally withdrawn from front-line squadrons until mid-1916, but by then it was being used mainly for reconnaissance, artillery observation and occasional escort work.

A B.E. reconnaissance machine flying over the trenches on the Western Front. From the outset, reconnaissance aircraft of the R.F.C. performed invaluable service in France and virtually became the eyes of the Army, reporting enemy troop movements and spotting for the artillery.     [*I.W.M.*

Another valuable tool for observation of the battlefield was the Cacqot kite balloon. Here two R.F.C. officers are seen in the basket of such a balloon. Note telephone, map rest and static-line-type parachutes.

Bristol Scout C No. 1255 of the R.N.A.S. making the first flight by a normal landplane from the deck of a British carrier—the seaplane carrier H.M.S. *Vindex* —on November 3, 1915. Pilot was S. Sub-Lt. H. F. Towler. The *Vindex* was originally an Isle of Man steamer—one of several converted into seaplane carriers for the R.N.A.S.

R.N.A.S. Coastal type non-rigid airship escorting a convoy. Coastal type airships, deliveries of which began in late 1915, were used for patrols off Lands End, the mouths of the Humber and the Forth, north of Aberdeen and off the Norfolk Coast.          [*I.W.M.*

The R.F.C.'s first single-seat fighter was the 93 m.p.h. D.H.2, powered by a 100 h.p. Gnome Monosoupape rotary engine and armed with a fixed, forward-firing Lewis gun.  Machines of this type first reached the Western Front in February 1916 and were largely responsible for ending the so-called 'Fokker scourge'.  Picture shows a D.H.2 taking off from Beauval aerodrome (No. 4 Army Aircraft Park).  Note the flag on the wing strut, indicating that it is a flight commander's machine.          [*I.W.M.*

*Above:* Carrier pigeons played a vital role in the 1914-18 War—as they did again in the Second World War. Pictures show a pigeon being released by an R.N.A.S. pilot while standing on the float of his Sopwith Baby seaplane and (*below*) an airman releasing a pigeon while his machine is in flight.

[*Upper photo I.W.M*

Food from the air.    In March and April, 1916, No. 30 Squadron R.F.C. was engaged in the
first air transport support operation in the history of British service flying.   This was during the
seige of Kut-el-Amara, Mesopotamia, when the squadron's B.E.2c's dropped supplies to the
British garrison.   Food was carried in 50 lb. bags slung on each side of the aircraft fuselages and
in 25 lb. bags fixed to the undercarriages (see photo).   Other supplies included medical comforts,
wireless parts, mail, currency and a 70 lb. millstone.   Naval aircraft were also employed;
altogether 140 food-dropping sorties were made and 19,000 lb. of food dropped.   The food-laden
aircraft, barely controllable owing to the head resistance which drastically reduced their normal
cruising speed of about 70 m.p.h., were attacked by German fighters, and towards the end of the
operation armed escort aircraft accompanied them.                                      [I.W.M.

A Farman M.F.11 bomber/reconnaissance aircraft in service with the R.F.C. in Mesopotamia.
                                                                                       [I.W.M.

R.F.C. personnel stationed at Castle Bromwich prepare Sunday lunch in a field kitchen.  The double-breasted tunics worn by R.F.C. personnel were universally known as 'maternity jackets'.

The 250 h.p. Short Bomber, landplane adaptation of the Short Type 184 seaplane, and one of the types used by No. 3 Wing R.N.A.S.—Britain's first strategic bombing force—at Luxeuil-les-Bains for long-range bombing attacks on Germany in 1916/17.  Carrying a crew of two, it had a maximum bomb load of 920 lb. and a maximum endurance of six hours.

[*I.W.M.*

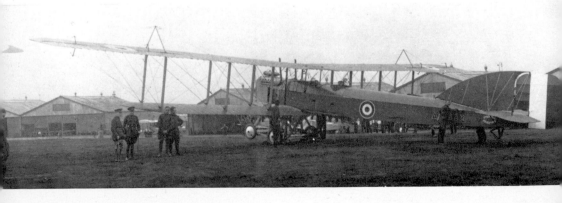

Another type used by No. 3 Wing, R.N.A.S.—and indeed widely used by both the R.N.A.S. and the R.F.C.—was the Sopwith 1½-Strutter. This was the first British aircraft already fitted with a synchronised front gun before it entered service (which it did early in 1916) and it could be flown as a standard bomber or reconnaissance two-seater, or as a single-seat bomber. Picture shows one of No. 3 Wing's two-seaters. [*I.W.M.*

Excitement at the R.N.A.S. Station, Coudekerque, France, on first sight of an O/100, Handley Page's answer to Cdre. Murray Sueter's famous request for a 'bloody paralyser'. O/100's first went into action in the spring of 1917.

Units of the R.F.C. also served on the North-West Frontier of India during the 1914-18 War. A B.E.2c leaves the camp at Tank on March 11, 1917 during operations against the Mahsuds.

[*I.W.M.*

An F.E.2b night bomber of No. 100 Squadron—the first British night bomber squadron—ready to leave its airfield in France on a raid. In October 1917 this squadron became one of the original units of the 41st Wing, R.F.C.—the bombing force which, in June 1918, became the Independent Force, R.A.F., and made many raids on targets in Germany.

[*I.W.M.*

An S.S.Z. (Sea Scout Zero) non-rigid naval airship, an improved version of the S.S. (Sea Scout) airships of 1915, and originally intended for towing by ships of the Belgian Coast Patrol and by monitors to assist gunnery spotting. Some 66 airships of this type were delivered in all, the first being flown to St. Pol (Dunkirk) in September 1916.

A special place in the history of the Service is enjoyed by the Avro 504, a war-time variant of which (a 504J) is seen here. The 504 was the first aeroplane to be delivered to the R.F.C. by a private constructor in 1912, and was used at the beginning of the 1914-18 War on active service in France. In 1917, in its 'J' form, it became the chosen instrument of the School of Special Flying at Gosport under Col. Smith-Barry and Maj. F. P. Scott. Final wartime variant was the 504K (some of which served as single-seat fighters with Home Defence squadrons), but a post-war model—the 504N—remained in service as a trainer until the early 1930s.

Royal visit to the R.F.C. in France. (*Above*) H.M. Queen Mary, accompanied by General Trenchard, inspecting a Bristol F.2b two-seat fighter at St. Omer on July 5, 1917.                                    [*I.W.M.*

*Below:* H.M. King George V and H.R.H. the Prince of Wales at No. 4 Squadron's airfield near Cassel on July 6, 1917, inspecting one of the squadron's R.E.8s which had crashed out of control only a quarter of an hour earlier. The controls were damaged during a combat with two enemy aircraft, but although the R.E.8 was completely wrecked in an 80 m.p.h. landing, neither of the crew was injured.                                    [*I.W.M.*

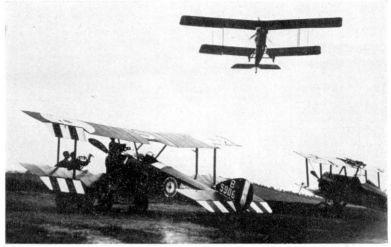

B.E.2e crazy-flying over a Sopwith Pup and a Sopwith F.1 Camel at Hainault Farm, Essex, in 1917.

By the end of the 1914-18 War over 100 aeroplanes had been allotted for use by ships of the Grand Fleet; each battleship and battle-cruiser was allocated a two-seat scout and a single-seat fighter. This illustration shows a Camel on a flying-off platform mounted over the forward gun turret of a light cruiser. No catapults were used in those days; the machines took off solely under their own power. [*I.W.M.*

Bristol Fighter with fabric removed to show interior of fuselage. Note Lewis gun ammunition drums and Very light cartridges.

An air mechanic handing photographic plates to an observer in an R.E.8 at an R.F.C. airfield near Arras on February 22, 1918. Affectionately known as the 'Harry Tate' (after the name of the famous contemporary music hall artist) the R.E.8 became one of the standard R.F.C./R.A.F. types of the latter half of the war. Its main duties, in addition to photo-reconnaissance, were artillery spotting and infantry contact patrol. Sometimes it was used for bombing.        [*I.W.M.*

Line-up of D.H.4 two-seat day bombers on the Western Front. Generally accepted as the best single-engined day bomber to serve with any of the combatants in the 1914-18 War, the D.H.4 was widely used not only by the R.A.F. and its predecessors, but also by the American Expeditionary Force. For the latter large quantities were built— with Liberty engines—in the U.S.A.

R.E.8 reconnaissance aircraft of No. 15 Squadron R.F.C. lined up by a roadside near Albert during the First Battle of Bapaume, March 25, 1918. [*I.W.M.*

Major General Sir Hugh Trenchard in 1918, the year in which he created the world's first independent air-striking force. Lord Trenchard, later first Marshal of the R.A.F., was the supreme architect of our modern air power and will be remembered forever as the 'Father of the R.A.F.'

On April 1, 1918—the day the R.A.F. was born—this picture was taken, showing a Bristol F.2B of No. 22 Squadron in flight over Vert Galand airfield, France. At dawn that day, 'Brisfits' of No. 22 Squadron made the first official sorties of the R.A.F. [*I.W.M.*

Cap badges of the R.F.C., R.N.A.S. (centre) and R.A.F. [*I.W.M.*

Two Handley Page O/100 heavy bombers on the airfield at Dunkirk, April 20, 1918. Similar machines, including the later O/400, were used by the Independent Force, based in the Nancy area of France, for long-range strategic night bombing attacks against targets in the Saar district of south-west Germany.

[*I.W.M.*

Air mechanics of No. 32 Squadron tuning-up an S.E.5a at Humiéres airfield, France, April 6, 1918. In the background are some Camels.

[*I.W.M.*

R.A.F. officers examining the fuselage of a captured Pfalz D.IIIa fighter at No. 2 Aircraft Depot at Candas, France, April 26, 1918.

[*I.W.M.*

View from the rear gunner's cockpit of a Handley Page bomber in flight, showing the two occupants of the pilot's cockpit and the forward observer, one of the engines and, in the background, another Handley Page. The aircraft belonged to No. 214 Squadron and were flying from the former R.N.A.S. airfield at Dunkirk on June 1, 1918.

[*I.W.M.*

*Left:* Mechanics refuel a Handley Page 0/400 of No. 214 Squadron at Dunkirk airfield, June 1, 1918.

[*I.W.M.*

*Right:* Pilot of an S.E.5a of No. 85 Squadron holding the unit's score-board, reading: 'Huns: 39 in 14 days', at St. Omer airfield, June 21, 1918.

[*I.W.M.*

*Left:* Pilots and observers of No. 22 Squadron at Serny, France, on June 17, 1918, hand over papers, etc., before going on patrol, to prevent useful information falling into enemy hands in the event of a forced landing. In the background are some of the squadron's Bristol Fighters.

[*I.W.M.*

*Right:* Officers and S.E.5a single-seat fighters of No. 1 Squadron at Clairmarais airfield, near St. Omer, France, on July 3, 1918. This is one of the comparatively few photographs of 1914-18 War squadron line-ups which escaped mutilation by the censor. Usually the aircrafts' serial numbers were scratched out on the negatives.

[*I.W.M.*

Pilot of an S.E.5a of No. 1 Squadron demonstrating how to fire the Lewis gun fitted to the Foster mounting on top of his machine. Clairmarais airfield, France, July 3, 1918.                    [*I.W.M.*

One of several F.E.2b night bomber squadrons which served on the Western Front in 1917-18 was No. 149 Squadron. Picture below shows a pilot and an observer watching a mechanic fuse a bomb under one of the Squadron's aircraft at Alquines airfield, near St. Omer, France, July 18, 1918. Note the flares beneath the F.E.'s wings.                    [*I.W.M.*

This tidy little lot of 112-pounder bombs was dropped by No. 149 Squadron's F.E.2b's in a single night in July 1918.

[*I.W.M.*

At nightfall the pilot and observer of an F.E.2b of No. 149 Squadron don their flying clothing in preparation for a mission.

[*I.W.M*

Damage to Valenciennes railway station, France, a frequent target for British bombers in the 1914-18 War.

[*I.W.M.*

(5  50  25)   W6180—778    20,000    9-16   HWV P1484/1)      Forms/W3348/2        Army Form W. 3348.
          10432 - M1079   50,000   11-16

# Combats in the Air.

Squadron: 45                                    Date: 27/9/17.

Type and No. of Aeroplane: Sopwith Camel B/3875        Time: 12.15 P.M.

Armament: 2 Vickers                             Duty: D.O.P.

Pilot: Capt.A.T.Harris                          Height: 10,000.

Observer: -

Locality: MOORSLEDE.

### Remarks on Hostile machine:—Type, armament, speed, etc.

7 Albatross Scouts.

### —— Narrative. ——

While getting height over POLYGON WOOD for a D.O.P. I saw 7 Albatross
Scouts between us and MOORSLEDE at our height.    We went over and attacked
them, chasing them E. of MOORSLEDE.    4 dived below us and I stalled and
dived right onto one underneath me, getting a burst of about 40 rounds into
him at 25 to 20 yards range.    He turned over at a very sharp angle and
dived vertically.    I immediately engaged a second Albatross Scout flying
100 yards East of me at my height: he turned eastwards and dived. I fired
about 20 rounds into him at 100 to 150 yards range.    The rest then sheered
off and I led the formation back to our lines, as, owing to the wind, it was
not advisable to remain in the locality.    I am certain the first machine
- or its pilot - was badly hit, but owing to the number of E.A. above and
around us I was unable to watch it crash.    The wind was too strong to
admit of us following them eastwards.

Among those who flew Camels on the Western Front was Capt. A. T. Harris,
now Marshal of the R.A.F. Sir Arthur T. Harris and Bomber Command's most
famous wartime A.O.C.-in-C.   Here is one of his combat reports from the
archives of No. 45 Squadron, which unit he was destined to command in the
1920s.                                                          [I.W.M.

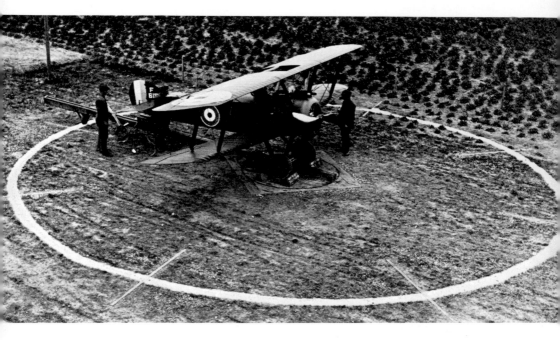

*Below:* Wet work : A 2F.1 Camel on a lighter, with a 30 ft. flying-off platform, being towed at speed behind a destroyer.    On August 11, 1918, Lt. S. D. Culley took off in a Camel from a towed lighter and destroyed the Zeppelin *L.53* off Terschelling. Through his glasses Rear Admiral Tyrwhitt watched the action and, as the airship fell in flames, instructed his Flag Lieutenant to make this signal : 'Flag—general : your attention is called to Hymn No. 224, verse 7'. Feverish reference to *Hymns Ancient and Modern* disclosed :

*O happy band of pilgrims,
Look upward to the skies,
Where such a light afflic-
    tion
Shall win so great a prize.*

Culley's Camel, which ditched in the sea after the action, is now preserved in the Imperial War Museum.

*Above:* Adjusting the compass of an F.1 Camel on a revolving table at the aircraft repair depot at Rang-du-Fliers, France, on July 12, 1918.  The Camel was probably the finest fighter of the 1914-18 War—Allied or enemy— and was undisputed champion in terms of enemy aircraft destroyed, its tally during only sixteen months of operations being 1,294 victories.                    [*I.W.M.*

*Above:* Air mechanics working on damaged fuselages at an aircraft repair depot near Rang-du-Fliers, July 12, 1918. Damaged aeroplanes were rebuilt at these depots and re-issued to the mobile supply parks nearer the front line.

[*I.W.M.*

*Left:* Largest bomb dropped on the Germans during the 1914-18 War was the 1,650-pounder, an example of which is seen here in front of a Handley Page O/400 of No. 207 Squadron, at Ligescourt, France, August 29, 1918. This particular bomb was reportedly dropped on Le Cateau railway station on the night of September 13/14, 1918.

[*I.W.M.*

The padré takes over: A now-famous photograph showing an R.A.F. padré conducting a Sunday morning service from the gunner's cockpit of an F.E.2b night bomber at No. 2 Aeroplane Supply Depot in France on September 1, 1918.

[*I.W.M.*

The observer and pilot in a Handley Page twin-engined heavy bomber photographed at an airfield near Cressy, France, on September 25, 1918.

[*I.W.M.*

*Above:* A night-flying F.1 Camel of 'C' Flight, No. 112 Home Defence Squadron, R.A.F., at Harrietsham, Kent. Note that the white circle has been painted out of the roundels. The pilot is Lt. A. S. C. Irwin, with his two dogs, Tinker and Pip. [*I.W.M.*

*Right:* In the summer of 1918 experiments were made to provide Britain's rigid airships with adequate means of defence against enemy aeroplanes. It was intended that an airship should carry a single-seat fighter which could be released and flown when the need arose. The first experiments were conducted at Pulham, Norfolk, using the airship R.23 and a 2F.1 Camel (see illustration) but although they were successful the Armistice removed the need for such devices. [*I.W.M.*

*Above:* Wreckage of a Zeppelin brought down over England. During the 1914-18 War, German airships made 51 raids on Great Britain while German aeroplanes made 52 raids. The bombs dropped—from airships 196 tons, and from aeroplanes 73 tons—killed 1,414 and injured 3,416 persons. Ten airships were brought down, eight by aeroplanes and two by anti-aircraft fire; and twenty-two German aeroplanes, nine by aircraft and thirteen by anti-aircraft fire.    *[I.W.M.*

*Right:* Bristol Fighters of No. 39 Home Defence Squadron. The Brisfit equipped three H.D.Squadrons; it was fitted with a ring sight (on the top centre section) set to face forward at an elevation of 45 degrees from the pilot's eye. The rear gunner fired over the pilot's head, at the same elevation, while the pilot aimed the aircraft, and at 100 m.p.h. the trajectory remained straight for 800 yards.

*Left:* Night-fighting version of the Sopwith Snipe for Home Defence duties. Note the modified roundels.

*Below:* Supporting the R.F.C., R.N.A.S. and R.A.F. in the 1914-18 War there grew up a great industry, employing in 1918 a total of nearly 350,000 men and women. It produced 26,685 aircraft and 29,561 engines in the last six months of the war alone. Here the ladies help prepare a Sopwith Salamander trench-strafer for the R.A.F. in 1918.

A Felixstowe F.2A flying-boat. Most famous of the series of Felixstowe 'boats, the F.2A was a redesign of the mediocre Curtiss H.12 undertaken by Sqn. Cdr. John C. Porte of the R.N.A.S. Almost 100 F.2As were built before the Armistice and the type was responsible for several U-boat and Zeppelin 'kills' in the North Sea area. *Below:* Cockpit of an F.2A.

In September 1918, R.A.F. aircraft of the Palestine Brigade played a major part in the final rout of the Turkish Seventh and Eighth Armies in Palestine. Their bombing and machine-gun attacks wrought frightful havoc on the luckless enemy troops and horses retreating along the Nablus-Beisan road, which ran through a deep defile known as the Wadi el Far'a. Here is part of the scene photographed on September 20. [*I.W.M.*

*R31*, one of several large rigid airships built for the Navy during the latter part of the 1914-18 War and the immediate post-war period. Of wooden construction, *R.31* was built by Shorts and first flew in August 1918, but suffered from various teething troubles. After being docked in a shed at Howden, Yorks, whose roof had been burned out when *R.27* caught fire three months earlier, it warped beyond repair. Airships remained under Naval control until December 1919 when all air units were transferred to the R.A.F. For economy reasons, the Airship Branch of the R.A.F. was closed down in the early 1920s but it later reformed for a brief period—until 1930, when airship development by Great Britain was abruptly ended by the *R.101* disaster. [*I.W.M.*

Soon after the Armistice—on December 13, 1918—the R.A.F. formed No. 1 (Communications) Squadron at Hendon to carry passengers and despatches between London and Paris during the Peace Conference. The Squadron was expanded into a Wing in January 1919 and continued to operate until September. At least three Handley Page O/400s, His Majesty's Air Liners *Great Britain, Silver Queen* and *Silver Star*, were converted into V.I.P. transports for use on this operation, each machine carrying six passengers. Their average time for the journey between the two capitals was 3 hr. 17 min., and their best time was 2 hr. 26 min. Photos show *Silver Star* with wings folded, and (*right*) cabin accommodation in *Great Britain*. The arrangement of the passenger accommodation in these two aircraft differed.

Another type used for cross-Channel services after the Armistice was the D.H.4. Some were flown by No. 2 (Communications) Squadron during the Peace Conference in 1919 and operated a daily return courier and mail service between the unit's base at Kenley and Buc, near Paris, average time for the journey being 2 hr. 10 min. Many cabinet ministers used the service, including Bonar Law and Winston Churchill. At Bonar Law's special request, several D.H.4s were modified to accommodate a minister and his secretary, sitting face to face in a glazed cabin, these being known as D.H.4a's, as shown *above* and *below*.

Sopwith Snipes of No. 70 Squadron at Bickendorf airfield, near Cologne, in March 1919. No. 70 was one of several R.A.F. units which served in Germany with the Army of Occupation.                                                    [*I.W.M.*

An illustration which speaks for itself. Alcock (left) and Brown, both ex-officers of the R.A.F., took off from Lester's Field, St. Johns, Newfoundland, in their specially-built Vimy and eventually landed in Derrygimla Bog, Clifden, Co. Galway, Ireland, covering the 1,890 miles in 16 hr. 12 min. Today their Vimy hangs for all to see in the Science Museum at South Kensington.

VICKERS-VIMY-ROLLS.
THE FIRST DIRECT FLIGHT ACROSS THE ATLANTIC.
JUNE. 14-15. 1919.
CAPT: SIR JOHN ALCOCK K.B.E. D.S.C.-PILOT.
LIEUT: SIR ARTHUR WHITTEN BROWN K.B.E-NAVIGATOR.

Two D.H.9a's and a Snipe at Bereznik airfield in August 1919, when British forces were serving in North Russia.

[*I.W.M.*

Mechanics of the Women's Royal Air Force working on the fuselage of an Avro 540, early postwar gunnery trainer version of the Avro 504K.   The W.R.A.F. was formed in April 1918 to effect the substitution of women for airmen in certain trades throughout the R.A.F., but was disbanded after the war.

[*I.W.M.*

Crew of a Handley Page V/1500 of No. 274 Squadron which, in August 1919, made a round-Britain flight in 12 hr. 28 min. The V/1500, or 'Super Handley' as it was sometimes known, was built originally to bomb Berlin and other enemy industrial centres from bases in England, but the Armistice came before it was able to go into action.

Snipes at the 1920 R.A.F. Pageant at Hendon. Eighteen R.A.F. Pageants and Displays were held at Hendon between the years 1920 and 1937, their purpose being to demonstrate the work and training of the R.A.F., for the benefit of Service charities.

Early in 1920 a small R.A.F. striking force called 'Z' Force operated in Somaliland against Mohammed bin Abdullah Hassan, known as the 'Mad Mullah'. An interesting innovation in these operations was the use for the first time in desert warfare of an aerial ambulance. This was a modified D.H.9 which carried a stretcher casualty and an attendant. Although there were no British casualties in action, there was some illness, and eight officers and airmen were evacuated from Eli dur Elan to Berbera by this method and thus saved a long and difficult journey. [*Top photo I.W.M.*

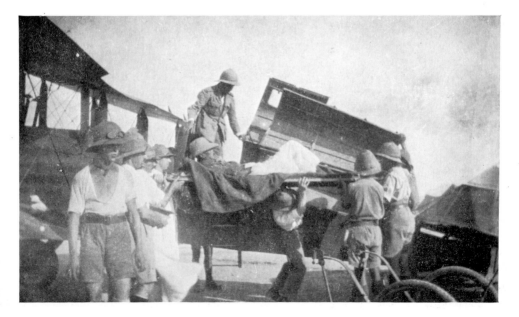

Felixstowe F.5 flying-boats on the slipway at Calshot. The F.5 was the standard flying-boat in service with the R.A.F. in the immediate post-war years. It was eventually replaced by the wooden-hulled Supermarine Southampton, first introduced in 1925.

When the Turko-Greek conflict, known as the Chanak crisis, began towards the end of 1922, the British garrison in Constantinople was immediately reinforced by R.A.F. units from England, Egypt and Malta. One squadron of Bristol Fighters, No. 4, travelled from England in H.M.S. *Ark Royal.* Owing to lack of disembarkation facilities at Kilia, the machines were transferred to H.M.S. *Argus* (photograph) and flown off its deck three days after arrival. Not one of the pilots had previously flown off a deck. [*I.W.M.*

One of a small number of Nieuport Nighthawk single-seat fighters which were purchased by the Air Ministry and allocated in 1923 to Nos. 1 and 8 Squadron in Mesopotamia for Service trials under tropical conditions.

Starting up a Snipe of No. 5 Flying Training School with a Hucks starter, 1925.

A Snipe of No. 5 Flying Training School. Contemporary air-to-air shots of Snipes are extremely rare and this example is one of the best that has so far come to light.

R.A.F. flying-boats on training sorties were a familiar sight at Britain's coastal resorts during the years between the two World Wars. Holidaymakers take a close look at a Supermarine Southampton I flying-boat of No. 480 Flight (Calshot) moored off Eastbourne on September 16, 1926.

Air and ground crew of a Vickers Vimy of No. 216 Squadron from Heliopolis, Egypt, pause for a meal during a desert landing ground survey. No. 216 was one of the squadrons which, during the 1920s, operated the famous Cairo-to-Baghdad air mail service; initially it flew D.H.10s (*below*), changing over to Vimys in 1922.

Some of the Vickers Vernons used on the Cairo-Baghdad air mail service.
Note the swastikas beneath the wings of the two machines nearest the
camera.

This Vickers Vernon ambulance aircraft was operated in Iraq by No. 45
Squadron.  Its pilot was Basil Embry (now Air Chief Marshal Sir Basil Embry),
who has vividly recorded something of No. 45's activities in his autobiography
*Mission Completed.*  The machine is seen flying over the Tigris.

Loading a stretcher case into a Vickers Vernon ambulance aircraft in the Middle East during the 1920s.

Blackburn Dart single-seat carrier-borne torpedo bomber exercising off Malta. This type entered service in 1923 and, although it did not possess a high performance, it contributed towards the technique of torpedo dropping. Its good deck-landing qualities are emphasised by the fact that on July 1, 1926, Flt. Lt. Boyce made the first night landing on board an aircraft carrier (H.M.S. *Furious*) whilst flying a Dart. The last Darts were retired from F.A.A. service in 1933.

One of our lesser-known aeroplanes, the Woodcock, which equipped two
R.A.F. squadrons in the 'twenties, was the Hawker Company's first single-seat
fighter.  In 1925-26 it replaced the Snipes of Nos. 3 and 17 Squadrons and
it was succeeded in turn in 1928 by Gamecocks in No. 3, and by Siskins in
No. 17.  Picture shows a Vic of three Woodcocks of No. 3 Squadron getting
airborne at Upavon.

D.H.9As of No. 207 Squadron at Eastchurch, Kent.  The 'Ninak' was the
standard day bomber both at home and overseas until the late 1920s.  In
addition to serving with Regular R.A.F. squadrons it also served with Auxiliary
squadrons.

The R.A.F. plays Santa Claus.  The 'sleigh' in this delightful study is a D.H.9A
of No. 47 Squadron, and the time and place Helwan, Egypt, December 1926.

[*C. A. Sims*

'Ninaks' of No. 60 Squadron at Kohat on the North West Frontier of India lined up in January 1927 for inspection by the visiting A.O.C., whose machine is seen in the background.                [*Gp. Capt. F. L. Newall*

Not all flights end in a perfect landing, even today. Here is an example of a landing that went wrong in the Middle East in the 1920s—featuring a Vickers Vernon bomber transport, probably of No. 45 Squadron.

Another prang.   Airmen in Iraq, wearing the famous 'Baghdad bowlers' of the period, examine a crashed D.H.9A of No. 30 Squadron in the 1920s. The device painted on the 'Ninak's' nose indicates that it is a machine of 'A' Flight.

A Bristol F.2.B of No. 208 Squadron in the Middle East in the late 1920s. The 'Biff' or 'Brisfit' as it was affectionately known, was the mainstay of the R.A.F.'s army co-operation units in the lean years which followed the 1914-18 War and did splendid work both at home and overseas. Later it served as a dual-control trainer at Cranwell and with the University Air Squadrons.

[*C. A. Sims*

One of the ugliest aeroplanes ever used by the R.A.F. was the Blackburn fleet spotter-reconnaissance machine, which served with the Fleet Air Arm from 1923 to 1931. It was powered by a 450 h.p. Napier Lion engine but, not surprisingly, its 'built-in headwind' limited its top speed to 100 m.p.h.

[*Aeroplane*

Standard front-line fighter of the Fleet Air Arm from 1923 to 1934 was the Fairey Flycatcher. This type served in all aircraft carriers of its day and was the last fighter to be flown from gun turrets of capital ships. Its design did not include folding wings, but the airframe could be dismantled for stowage. *Above:* A 'slip flight' Flycatcher gets away from the forward hangar of H.M.S. *Glorious.* *Below:* A Flycatcher amphibian takes off from the sea at Singapore.

[*Upper photo: Flight International*

Fairey Fawn—probably of No. 100 Squadron—about to have its propeller swung by a Hucks starter in the 1920s. The Fawn entered R.A.F. service in 1924 and was the first new type of light day bomber in the period of stringent financial economies which followed the 1914-18 War. It eventually equipped five squadrons.

A Supermarine Seagull III of No. 440 (Fleet Reconnaissance) Flight, F.A.A., flying over Malta in 1927. Only a few of these three-seat amphibians were built for the F.A.A. and, after service in H.M.S. *Eagle* and on the Mediterranean station, the class disappeared for a decade until revived in the shape of the Walrus.

*Right:* Fairey IIID seaplane over Malta. The IIID entered service in 1924 and was the general-purpose seaplane of the R.A.F. for many years, being used mainly by the F.A.A. Some IIID's—the minority—were operated as landplanes.

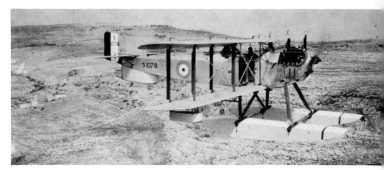

*Below:* In 1925 the Fairey Company produced, as a private venture, the revolutionary Fox two-seat day bomber. Owing to its clean aerodynamic form—made possible by the use of a Curtiss D.12 engine of low frontal area—the Fox advanced the speed of R.A.F. day bombers by 50 m.p.h.; indeed, for a while, it outpaced the R.A.F.'s first-line fighters. Lord Trenchard personally ordered sufficient Foxes to equip a squadron—No. 12—which subsequently adopted a fox's mask as its badge and 'Leads the Field' as its motto. Photo shows machines of No. 12 Squadron in flight.

*Left:* This Hawker Woodcock of No. 17 Squadron was loaned to America's Colonel Lindbergh on June 2, 1927, to enable him to return to Paris from London by air soon after his famous solo transatlantic flight in the Ryan monoplane *Spirit of St. Louis.*

*Below:* The Supermarine S.5, N219, of the R.A.F. High Speed Flight, which gained second place in the 1927 Schneider Trophy Contest at Venice, with an average speed of 273.07 m.p.h.; pilot was Flt. Lt. O. E. Worsley. A sister-aircraft, numbered N220 and flown by Flt. Lt. N. Webster, won the 1927 Contest by averaging 281.65 m.p.h.

The wonder of it all. Children admire a Handley Page Hyderabad of No. 99 Squadron which forced-landed in a beet field at Mistley. It developed engine trouble while flying, at midnight, 10,000 ft. over Clacton-on-Sea during the Air Exercises in the summer of 1927. The crew of four were uninjured.

Aerial view of R.A.F. Station Upper Heyford, Oxon, on the opening day, January 1, 1928. In the years up to the war, it was the home of many well-known bomber squadrons including No. 99, first to fly the famous Handley Page Heyford night bomber, which was so named in the Station's honour.

Hawker Horsley day bombers fly over bus loads of Halton apprentices at the 1928 R.A.F. Display. Used by the R.A.F. as both a day bomber and a torpedo bomber, the Horsley replaced the Fawns in Nos. 11 and 100 Squadrons in 1927, while the first torpedo bomber versions went to No. 36 Squadron in 1928. The last frontline day bomber and torpedo bomber Horsleys were withdrawn in 1934 and 1935 respectively.
[Aeroplane

The first major airlift in history was organised by the R.A.F. during the rebellion in Afghanistan in the winter of 1928-29. R.A.F. aircraft, operating from India—mainly Vickers Victorias of No. 70 Squadron—rescued 586 people, including the Afghan royal family, from Kabul under the barrels of the rebel guns; they also carried 24,193 lb. of luggage. In two months they flew more than 28,000 miles over mountains averaging 10,000 ft., in some of the worst weather on record.

The Victorias in the Kabul airlift were supplemented by the prototype Handley Page Hinaidi, the only other twin-engined machine involved, seen here over Delhi in 1930 while it was still in India on service evaluation trials. Production versions of the Hinaidi replaced the Hyderabads of Nos. 10 and 99 Squadrons in the U.K. and also served with two cadre squadrons of the Special Reserve.

This dual-control trainer version of the Gloster Grebe—one of the R.A.F.'s standard fighters of the 1930s—piloted by Flt. Lt. R. L. R. Atcherley and navigated by Flt. Lt. G. H. Stainforth, won the 1929 King's Cup Air Race. There were 41 starters and Atcherley's machine averaged 150.3 m.p.h. Atcherley (now Air Marshal Sir Richard) and Stainforth both members of that year's Schneider Trophy Team.

Developed for the 1929 Schneider Trophy Contest, the Gloster VI, or Golden Arrow, was one of the most beautiful aeroplanes ever flown. Two were built and just three days after the 1929 Schneider Trophy Contest the machine illustrated set a new world speed record of 336.31 m.p.h., with a maximum speed on one run of 351.6 m.p.h.; however, this was beaten only a few hours later by a Supermarine S.6.
[C. A. Sims

Troops emplaning in a Vickers Victoria in the Middle East and (*below*) the interior of a Victoria showing the folding canvas seats. The Victoria was flown by a crew of two and could accommodate 22 troops.

'War games' marking on an Armstrong Whitworth Atlas army co-operation machine. The Atlas, in 1927, was the first aircraft to enter R.A.F. service which had been designed for army co-operation work from the outset. Such work had been performed hitherto by a specially adapted version of the veteran Bristol Fighter.

Gloster Grebes of No. 22 Squadron—then part of the Aeroplane and Armament Experimental Establishment, and never a first-line Grebe unit—trailing coloured smoke at the 1930 Hendon Air Display. A single-seat fighter, the Grebe entered R.A.F. squadron service in 1924 and made history at the 1925 Hendon Display when a No. 25 Squadron formation team, led by Sqn. Ldr. A. H. Peck, used ground-to-air and aircraft-to-aircraft R/T. It was the first public demonstration of ground control of an R.A.F. formation and King George V, speaking to Sqn. Ldr. Peck over the radio, made a request for a manoeuvre of his own choosing—which the formation promptly executed. Part of the R/T conversation was broadcast by the B.B.C. over Station 2LO.

Fairey Flycatchers of No. 405 Flight, H.M.S. *Glorious,* flying in Vic formation. The Flycatcher was an extremely manoeuvrable aeroplane and in a dive its noise was rivalled only by that of the Harvard of more recent times. Those who remember the Harvard can well imagine what this little lot might have sounded like in a dive!

A Parnall Peto being catapulted from the submarine *M.2* in the late 'twenties. This small two-seat reconnaissance aircraft was designed specially to operate from *M.2,* in which hangar accommodation was provided. The first two pilots to fly a Peto on board the submarine (Lt. C. W. Byas and Lt. C. Keighley-Peach) received both flying and submarine pay! The submarine/aircraft experiment was not a success, and was not pursued after the loss of the *M.2* off Weymouth.

Showing the flag—literally.  Four Fairey IIIFs of No. 47 Squadron, which made one of the early Cairo-to-The Cape training flights in the late 1920s. (*Below*) Close-up of the C.O.'s machine, showing the R.A.F. ensign and the Squadron Leader's pennant.

*Above:* The pilot of an Armstrong Whitworth Siskin IIIA fighter wearing an electrically-heated suit for high flying. Electrically-heated flying clothing was not unknown in the 1914-18 War, although it seems that it was used mainly by our bomber crews—and only in the final stages of the war.

[*Charles E. Brown*

*Below right:* The Siskin was the standard R.A.F. fighter in the late 1920s, no fewer than 11 squadrons eventually equipping with it. For aerobatics it was superb and probably the most memorable of its many R.A.F. Display performances was that of 1930, when No. 43 Squadron's Siskin IIIA's, led by Sqn. Ldr. C. N. Lowe, flew in formation and did aerobatics with the three aircraft of each flight tied together with rubber cords to which were attached little flags (*see photo*). Although this was not, as is sometimes claimed, a completely new tactic (the U.S. Army Air Service having done aerobatics with one formation of aircraft linked in this way at Dayton, Ohio, in October, 1924) it was the first time that three formations had performed tied-together aerobatics at a public display.

[*Flight International*

'Crazy flying' act by two Avro 504Ns at the 1930 Hendon Display. Piloting one of the Avros was P/O Frank Whittle, now Air Cde. Sir Frank Whittle of jet-engine fame. Recalling the performance at Hendon in his autobiography *Jet*, he told how he afterwards learned that at least one spectator—an old lady—was not at all impressed. She was heard to comment to an excited small boy, 'There's nothing to get excited about—they haven't got far to fall!'

[*Aeroplane*

Vic of three Hawker Horsley torpedo bombers of No. 11 Squadron over the Firth of Forth in the early 'thirties. When No. 11 first had Horsleys it had a day-bombing role, and a curious thing about the unit is that, although it converted to the torpedo-bomber in 1930/31, its official designation was not changed from 'bomber' to 'torpedo bomber' until 1933.

[*Flight International*

Boulton Paul Sidestrand medium bombers of No. 101 Squadron—the only squadron thus equipped—flying in echelon formation in April 1931. The Sidestrand was remarkably manoeuvrable for a twin-engined machine and could be looped, spun and rolled without difficulty. Its aerobatic capacity was demonstrated in mock engagements with fighters at some of the Hendon Displays.

[*Flight International*

Royal Passenger. The Prince of Wales takes off from H.M.S. *Glorious* in a Fairey IIIF, bound for Malta.

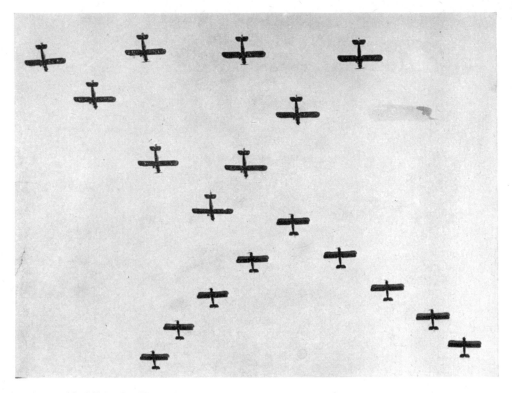

Air drill by Auxiliary Air Force Wapitis at one of the R.A.F. Displays at Hendon in the early 1930s.

Sqn. Ldr. P. Huskinson, in the rear cockpit of a Fairey IIIF of No. 24 (Communications) Squadron, prepares to shoot down his quarry during the 'big game hunt' at the 1931 Hendon Air Display.

Bit o' bull for a Bulldog. The R.A.F.'s biplane fighters of the 'thirties were noted for their highly-polished cowlings, and individual squadrons took a great pride in maintaining their machines in spotless condition. Here the C.O. of No. 32 Squadron looks on approvingly as the exhaust manifold of his Bristol Bulldog gets a final polish.

Bristol Bulldogs of No. 41 Squadron, Northolt. This pugnacious-looking single-seat fighter entered service in 1929 and by 1931 equipped nine squadrons, remaining the most widely-used R.A.F. fighter until 1936.

[*Aeroplane*

Cockpit of a Bristol Bulldog.

In the years between the two world wars, new aircraft designed for the R.A.F. and F.A.A. went to the Aeroplane and Armament Experimental Establishment—or Aeroplane Experimental Station as it was known prior to April 1924—at Martlesham Heath in Suffolk for service testing and evaluation. Among the many experimental prototypes that went there was this Vickers F.29/27 single-seat fighter, first flown in 1931, fitted with a Coventry Ordnance Works 37 mm shell-firing gun.

The two Supermarine S.6Bs and one S.6 of the 1931 Schneider Trophy Team at Calshot: left to right—Supermarine S.6B S1596 (Flt. Lt. Stainforth's record breaker), S.6 N248 (F/O Atcherley's 1929 machine) and S.6B S1595 (Flt. Lt. Boothman's winning machine). At Spithead on September 12, 1931, the Schneider Trophy was won outright by Great Britain with a third successive victory. The winning machine averaged 340·6 m.p.h. On September 29 the other S.6B, with its engine boosted to 2,600 h.p., was flown by Flt. Lt. Stainforth at 407·5 m.p.h., thus gaining the world's speed record for Great Britain. The S.6B was the first aircraft in the world to exceed 400 m.p.h.     *[Flight International*

An Armstrong Whitworth Siskin IIIA of No. 29 (Fighter) Squadron has its radio equipment tested before taking off to participate in the Air Defence Exercises in July 1931.

The interceptor. Classic study of a Hawker Fury I of No. 43 Squadron—the famous 'Fighting Cocks'. This superbly-proportioned and highly-aerobatic machine was the first R.A.F. fighter in squadron service to exceed 200 m.p.h., and No. 43 was the first unit to be so equipped—in May and June 1931. Two more squadrons flew Fury Is—Nos. 1 and 25—and the type remained in first-line service until 1939 when it was superseded by the Hurricane.

[*Aeroplane*

Hawker Harts of Nos. 11 and 39 Squadrons of No. 2 (Indian) Wing, flying at 20,000 feet, cross the inhospitable Himalayas, *en route* from Risalpur to Gilgit in Kashmir on October 17, 1932. The 300-mile flight up the Indus and over the mountains to Gilgit was an annual event: the aircraft used to visit the Agency there and 'show the flag' to the local tribesmen.

R.A.F.'s first instrument flying trainers were six Avro 504Ns of 'E' Flight at the Central Flying School, Wittering (Northants), where the first course started in September 1931.   The Avros were rigged with one degree less dihedral, to reduce their inherent stability, and were fitted with blind-flying hoods and Reid and Sigrist turn and bank indicators.  Photograph shows one of the machines during a blind take-off.              [Charles E. Brown

Vickers Virginia X in flight.   The Virginia in its various versions was the mainstay of our night bombing squadrons for roughly a decade. The threat of war seemed remote during its lifetime and, as money for defence was scarce, it soldiered on as front-line equipment up to and beyond the time when its replacement, the Heyford, was introduced.  The two final versions, Mks. IX and X, were the first bombers in large-scale service to embody a gun position in the tail.                      [Charles E. Brown

Westland Wapiti of No. 55 Squadron over difficult country
for a forced-landing, in Kurdistan, 1932.

Inverted formation flying by these Tiger Moths of the
Central Flying School was one of the highlights of the
1931 Hendon Air Display. It took the pilots—instructors
on the staff of the C.F.S.—weeks of practice to learn
inverted formation flying and they could, if need be,
keep it up for a quarter of an hour or more.

[*Charles E. Brown*

A special feature of each year's Hendon Air Show was the new types park, in which the latest prototypes of military or pseudo-military aeroplanes were displayed. Here is an aerial view of the new types park at the 1932 Display, with the Fairey Hendon and the Handley Page Heyford among the trio of camouflaged night bombers seen in the foreground.

Auxiliary airmen of No. 600 (County of Middlesex) Squadron attach a bomb to a Wapiti at Hendon, under the vigilant eye of an R.A.F. Sergeant, during Air Exercises in the early 1930s.

A Vickers Valentia equipped with loudspeakers to assist in the control of native tribes.  For some years previously a Victoria had been used for 'sky-shouting', as it was known.  So successful was this, in operations in Iraq, that the Valentia was equipped with broadcasting apparatus with the idea of trying it out in other regions such as the North-West Frontier of India and Somaliland.

[*Charles E. Brown*

Fairey Seal spotter reconnaissance seaplane being hoisted on board H.M.S. *Valiant* in January 1933, in readiness for the Home Fleet's spring cruise into southern waters. The Seal was the F.A.A. equivalent of the R.A.F.'s Gordon and, like the latter, it served as both a landplane and a seaplane.

In February 1933 the Fairey Long Range Monoplane K1991 flew 5,341 miles non-stop from Cranwell to Walvis Bay, 781 miles north of Cape Town, in 57 hr. 25 min. This gained for Great Britain a world record for distance in a straight line (at that time, this country already held the world speed and aeroplane height records). Sqn. Ldr. O. R. Gayford was in command, with Flt. Lt. G. E. Nicholetts as second pilot and navigator. In April 1929 an earlier version of this aeroplane had made the first non-stop flight from England to India. In our photo K1991 is seen at Capetown.

About 50 dual-control Bulldogs were supplied to the R.A.F. for fighter training purposes. The one in the picture, which was probably taken in 1933, has F/O H. V. Satterley (now A.V.-M. Satterley) in the rear cockpit. He was then an instructor at Cranwell.

Under arrest. A Nimrod—naval counterpart of the R.A.F.'s Fury single-seat interceptor—of No. 800 Squadron seen at the moment of picking up the arrester wires on the deck of H.M.S. *Furious*.

[*Charles E. Brown*

Fine air-to-air study of two Supermarine Southampton II's. First post-war-designed flying-boat to enter service, the Southampton superseded the Felixstowe 'boats of 1918 vintage, the Mk. II being the major type. Southamptons served with the R.A.F. for more than a decade, being succeeded during 1935-36 by Londons, Rangoons and Singapores. Many notable flights were made by Southamptons, the most famous being the 28,000-mile cruise to Australia and Hong Kong in 1927-28, by four aircraft of the Far East Flight led by Group Capt. H. M. Cave-Browne-Cave. The cruise lasted 14 months and at the end of it the Far East Flight stayed in Singapore becoming, in January 1929, No. 205 Squadron.

[*Charles E. Brown*

Avro Tutors, flown by Central Flying School instructors, rehearsing their display of inverted flying and aerobatics which became a famous feature of the R.A.F. Hendon Air Display from 1933 onwards. The top surfaces of these single-seater Tutors were distinctively marked to indicate 'wrong side down!'

[*Charles E. Brown*

Bristol Bulldogs performing aerobatics, with smoke, at a Hendon Display in the mid-thirties.                                    [*Charles E. Brown*

Avro 504N's—or Lynx Avros as they were popularly known—of Cambridge University Air Squadron over Netheravon (Wilts.) in the 1930s during the annual training camp. This development of the wartime 504K was the first new trainer to be adopted by the R.A.F. after the 1914-18 War and it remained in production until 1932.                                   [*Charles E. Brown*

In their element. A Vickers Virginia X of No. 7 Squadron and
*below:* a Handley Page Heyford Ia of No. 10 Squadron.
These two types were the last of the big biplane bombers
to remain in squadron service with the R.A.F.  They were
still the mainstay of our heavy bomber force as late as 1937,
in which year they began to be supplanted by the Whitley,
first of the new generation of monoplane 'heavies' to enter
service.                                       [*Upper photo Flight International*

Wheels and floats: F/O J. B. T. Whitehead flying a No. 47 Squadron Fairey Gordon past Jebel Kassala in 1933. *Below:* Gordon floatplane of No. 47 Squadron alongside an Arab dhow on the Nile at Khartoum in 1934.

A de Havilland 60M Gipsy Moth of the Communications Flight at an advanced landing ground in the Aden Protectorate in the mid-1930s.

Two Hawker Harts of No. 33 Squadron flying over their base at Bicester (Oxon.) about 1934. No. 33 was the first squadron to receive this famous day bomber (in 1930). Three years later it was making news with dive-bombing trials which it was conducting against armoured launches, used as evading targets, in the Solent. It was the first time this bombing tactic had been tried seriously in the R.A.F. and it is recorded that one of the volunteer airmen employed as helmsmen on the target launches was Aircraftman Shaw—better known as Lawrence of Arabia.

*Above:* Hawker Audaxes, army co-operation machines—or ' 'arts with 'ooks' as they became in the playful language of the Service, for reasons which are all too obvious— flying low to pick up messages during an 'at home' at R.A.F. Andover (Hants.) in June 1934   The Audaxes bear the markings of No. 2 Squadron.

*Right top:* The Prince of Wales arrives by air at Cranwell (Lincs.) on October 11, 1934, to open the new main building at the R.A.F. College which the Air Ministry founded on the lines of Sandhurst and Woolwich to create an Air Force spirit and to train officers for permanent service.   Also shown in the picture are (left to right) Lord Londonderry (Secretary of State for Air), A.V.-M. G. S. Mitchell (first Commandant of the College) and Lord Yarborough (Lord Lieutenant of Lincolnshire).   The aircraft is a D.H. Dragon.

*Right bottom:* Hawker Osprey being catapulted from the cruiser H.M.S. *Neptune* during Home Fleet manoeuvres in the North Sea in August 1934.   From the mid-twenties until the Second World War, most cruisers and battleships of the Royal Navy carried catapult aircraft for reconnaissance purposes.

*Below:* Blackburn Perth on its way from Brough to the Marine Aircraft Experimental Establishment at Felixstowe, for Service trials before being posted to a squadron. Three Perths were built for the R.A.F. and the type, like its predecessor the Iris, was the Service's largest and fastest flying-boat, a distinction it retained until superseded in 1936 by the Short Singapore III.   A feature of the Perth was that it mounted in the bows a 37 mm automatic gun, which fired $1\frac{1}{2}$ lb. shells at the rate of 100 rounds per minute.

[*Charles E. Brown*

The R.A.F.'s first rotating-wing aircraft was the Cierva C.30 Autogiro, six of which were delivered to the School of Army Co-operation at Old Sarum (Wilts.) in December, 1934. A two-seater, powered by a 140 h.p. Armstrong Siddeley Genet Major engine, the C.30 was built under licence by Avro and known by the R.A.F. as the Rota.

Delightful study of three Vickers Valentia bomber transports of No. 216 Squadron, Heliopolis, flying over the Citadel, Cairo, during the mid-1930s.

[*Charles E. Brown*

Armoured cars played an important part in the R.A.F.'s policing of the Middle East in the years between the two world wars. *Above:* A convoy including two armoured cars pauses in the desert during a patrol. A Fairey Gordon flies overhead, the observer standing up in the rear cockpit to wave at the crews, *Below:* Another view of an armoured car. These vehicles were invariably named, this one being called 'Cerberus' after the mythical three-headed watch-dog of Hades.                    [*Upper photo  Charles E. Brown*

A Blackburn Baffin loses a tyre while landing on H.M.S. *Courageous.* The Baffin succeeded the Ripon as the standard torpedo bomber of the Fleet Air Arm, but was only slightly superior in performance and was itself soon supplanted by the Swordfish.

Lord Swinton, Secretary of State for Air, dons his parachute prior to a flight in a Hart of No. 24 Squadron.

Handley Page Heyford of No. 10 Squadron during an air gunnery exercise at the annual armament camp, North Coates Fitties (Lincs) in 1935.   The target drogue is seen below it.                                    [*Charles E. Brown*

Clutch of 'eggs' for a Heyford.

First R.A.F. bomber to incorporate a totally-enclosed power-operated gun turret was the Boulton Paul Overstrand, which served with No. 101 Squadron from 1935 until 1938. The Overstrand— which was developed from the Sidestrand—had a Boulton Paul turret mounting a single Lewis gun in a vertical slot. Rotation was by means of compressed air from storage bottles fed from an engine-driven compressor, and operation was automatic by pressing one or other side of the gun. By elevating the gun to 70° or more, in order to clear the fuselage side, the turret could be revolved continuously through 360°.

[Charles E. Brown

On retirement from first-line service—they were gradually replaced by Heyfords and Whitleys—Virginias ended their days at the Home Aircraft Depot, Henlow (Beds) where they were used for parachute training. Here a trainee has released his parachute and is being pulled off the special platform at the wing strut under the watchful eye of the instructor, who is sitting in front of him. Another trainee stands ready to make a 'pull-off' descent from the starboard wing.

[*Charles E. Brown*

Cross-fire: the air gunner of a Hart of No. 603 (City of Edinburgh) Squadron, Auxiliary Air Force, aims his camera-gun at a fighter 'attacking' another machine of the squadron.

[*Flight International*

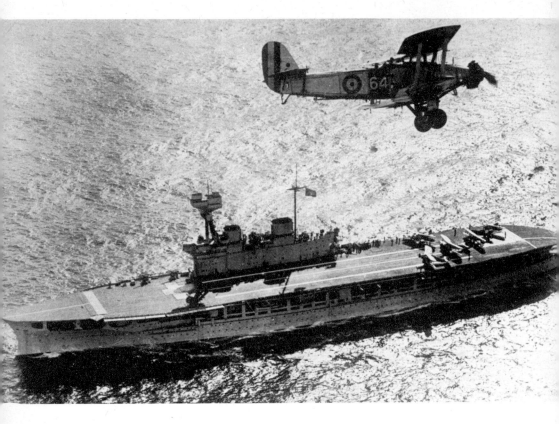

Blackburn Baffin torpedo bombers take off from H.M.S. *Eagle,* with the Mediterranean Fleet, during combined exercises of the Home ('Redland') and Mediterranean Fleet ('Blueland') in the spring of 1935.

Bristol Bulldogs of No. 3 Squadron, Kenley, practising aerobatics with smoke for the 1935 R.A.F. Display.                    [*Charles E. Brown*

A Westland Wallace and a Hawker Hart from the R.A.E., Farnborough, demonstrate in-flight refuelling at the 1935 R.A.F. Display.     [*Aeroplane*

View from pilot's cockpit of a Virginia bomber during the skittle-bombing contest at the 1935 R.A.F. Display at Hendon. Note the tail gunner out in the cold.     [*Aeroplane*

*Above:* Tiger with a difference. De Havilland Queen Bee, the radio-controlled target version of the Tiger Moth. First flown in 1935, this type was produced as both a landplane and a seaplane to provide live gunnery practice. Photograph shows the seaplane version being catapulted from a cruiser.

*Right:* A de Havilland Queen Bee radio-controlled target aircraft being demonstrated at Farnborough on June 26, 1935. The control desk had a series of push-buttons, each of which automatically sent out the code signal which produced a certain manoeuvre. The buttons included those for left turn, right turn, straight flight, climb, dive and level flight.    [*Aeroplane*

Gloster Gauntlets of No. 19 Squadron practise formation flying above the clouds over Duxford (Cambs) for H.M. King George V's Jubilee Review of the R.A.F. in 1935.   Last of the R.A.F.'s open-cockpit fighter biplanes, the Gauntlet equipped 17 R.A.F. or Auxiliary squadrons—many of them formed under the Expansion Scheme—during the period 1935-39.   An interesting sideline on its career is that it was the first R.A.F. fighter to make an interception whilst directed by ground radar.   This historic moment came in November 1937, when machines of No. 32 Squadron, Biggin Hill, were vectored by radar at Bawdsey Manor on to an in-bound civil airliner over the Thames.

*[Charles E. Brown*

Three Kings.   Under the nose of a Handley Page Heyford night bomber of No. 99 Squadron are three Kings of England—George V, Edward VIII (then Prince of Wales) and George VI (Duke of York at the time).   The occasion was the Jubilee Review of the R.A.F. at Mildenhall on July 6, 1935.   Later that day the Heyfords of Nos. 99 and 10 Squadrons led the mass fly-past which was staged at Duxford.

Aircraft lined up at Mildenhall for the Jubilee Review.
[*Charles E. Brown*

Harts of No. 601 (County of London) Squadron, Auxiliary
Air Force, liveried as fighters, in 1935, some months after
the squadron assumed a fighter role. These makeshift
fighters of No. 601 were eventually replaced by Demons.
[*Charles E. Brown*

The expansion of the R.A.F., which began in November 1934, created many new bomber squadrons, albeit with no really modern aircraft types to equip them. As an interim measure, orders were placed for a Hart variant, the Hawker Hind, pending the introduction of the Fairey Battle and Bristol Blenheim. The Hind began to enter service during the winter of 1935-36 and our photograph shows a machine of No. 57 Squadron, which received the type in May 1936.

[*Aeroplane*

Vickers Vincent general-purpose aircraft of No. 207 Squadron over the Egyptian Desert in 1936. Replacing the Wapiti and IIIF, the Vincent was a modified version of the Vildebeeste torpedo bomber, with a long-range fuel tank slung beneath its fuselage, a message pick-up hook and special equipment for operations in tropical climates. It entered R.A.F. squadron service in 1935 and was used in the Middle East.       [*Charles E. Brown*

A Vincent—probably of No. 8 Squadron—loaded with bombs for operations against dissident tribesmen in the Middle East in 1936.

No. 102 Squadron's Handley Page Heyford night bombers at the newly-constructed airfield at Finningley (Yorks) in 1936, a few months after the unit had been re-formed under the R.A.F. Expansion Scheme. In December 1936 No. 102 suffered what amounted in peacetime to a major disaster, when seven Heyfords *en route* from Aldergrove, Northern Ireland, to Finningley encountered dense fog and severe icing conditions over England. Only one machine managed to reach its destination; three crashed (one having first been abandoned by its crew when it became uncontrollable), and three forced-landed. Three airmen were killed and three were injured.      [*Charles E. Brown*

Blackburn Sharks flying in echelon port formation. The Shark was the last of the line of Blackburn torpedo biplanes for the Fleet Air Arm and had but a brief spell of first-line service, being superseded within less than four years by the Swordfish. That was in 1938, by which time the F.A.A. was in the process of reverting to Admiralty control.                    [*Charles E. Brown*

Hawker Demons of No. 600 (City of London) Squadron, Auxiliary Air Force. The Demon was derived from the Hart day bomber, and its entry into service in 1933 revived in the R.A.F. the two-seat fighter, a class which had been absent since the 1914-18 War.                    [*Flight International*

Short Singapore III of No. 209 Squadron, Mount Batten
(near Plymouth), setting out on an anti-piracy patrol on
September 18, 1937, during the Spanish Civil War.


Loading up a Singapore III with practice bombs.

Supermarine Scapas of No. 202 Squadron over Alexandria
Harbour. The Scapa was produced in the early 1930s as a
completely modernised, re-engined version of the Southampton III, and was known originally as the Southampton
IV. *[Charles E. Brown*

Scapa of No. 202 Squadron, Kalafrana, Malta, refuelling
from the depot ship *Pass of Balmaha* in 1936.

Supermarine Stranraer being lowered on to the water by a giant crane at Felixstowe (Suffolk). Last of a long line of biplane 'boats designed by R. J. Mitchell, of Schneider Trophy racer and Spitfire fame, the Stranraer entered R.A.F. service in 1936. Unlike its contemporaries, the London and Singapore, it was used exclusively by home-based squadrons of Coastal Command and did not serve overseas.                                    [*Aeroplane*

Pranged on delivery. The first Bristol Blenheim to be flown to a squadron—K7036—was wrecked on arrival at Wyton (Hunts) when the pilot braked too hard, causing it to ground loop, March 10, 1937.

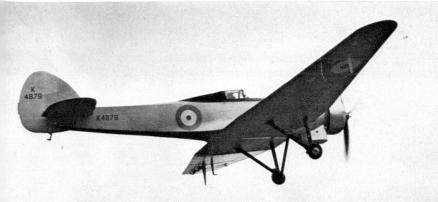

In June 1937 Great Britain regained the world's height record for heavier-than-air craft when Flt. Lt. M. J. Adam, of the Royal Aircraft Establishment, Farnborough, reached a height of 53,937 ft. in this all-wooden Bristol 138 monoplane powered by a special Bristol Pegasus engine with a two-stage supercharger. Great Britain had previously gained the record in September 1936, with the Bristol 138 when, piloted by Sqn. Ldr. F. R. D. Swain, it reached 49,967 ft. This record was broken by Italy in May 1937, at a height of 51,362 ft., but in the following month Flt. Lt. Adam regained the record for this country. *Below:* Special pressurised suit worn by the pilot of the Bristol 138—in this instance Sqn. Ldr. Swain. 

[*Aeroplane*

Four Hawker Fury Is of No. 1 Squadron's famous aerobatic team photographed in 1937. The team's Furys were star performers at air displays in the 1930s, and in 1937, a few weeks after participating in the final pre-war R.A.F. Display, they visited the Zurich International Air Meeting, gaining further acclaim.     [*Charles E. Brown*

*Left:* Three Gloster Gladiators of No. 87 Squadron practising tied-together aerobatics above the clouds during the summer of 1937. Last of the R.A.F.'s biplane fighters, the four-gun Gladiator first entered service with No. 3 Squadron at Tangmere (Sussex) in February 1937.

*Below:* Fury IIs of No. 25 Squadron, Hawkinge (Kent) flying in Vic formation. This type first entered service early in 1937 and, although it eventually equipped five squadrons, its operational career was brief. By 1939 it had withdrawn completely from front-line service, being replaced by Gladiators, Hurricanes and Spitfires.

[*Aeroplane*

Although the R.A.F. began its vast expansion programme in 1934, it took a long time to replace with modern monoplanes the biplanes then in service. As a result, when the front-line squadrons were put on show at the 1937 Hendon Air Display, some critics implied that little progress had been made since the days of the 20-year-old Maurice Farman which flew overhead.

[*Charles E. Brown*

The future enemy takes a look. A German air mission, headed by Gen. Milch, inspects Heyford bombers during a visit to Mildenhall (Suffolk) in October 1937. At that date the Heyford still formed the backbone of our bomber force.

Hendon heavy night bomber.  The Hendon was the first all-metal low-wing cantilever monoplane to enter R.A.F. squadron service.  All of the 14 production models were allotted to No. 38 Squadron at Mildenhall and, later, Marham, between November 1936 and July 1937.

Fitter at work on the Merlin engine of a Fairey Battle day bomber.

Bombing-up a Handley Page Harrow of No. 115 Squadron with 250-pounders at Marham (Norfolk) in 1937 or '38. Conceived as a transport, the Harrow was used as an interim bomber and entered service in 1937. It was replaced in the bomber squadrons by the Wellington in 1939 and served during the war in its originally-intended transport role.

Vickers Wellesley two-seat long-range day bombers of No. 148 Squadron at Scampton (Lincs) in 1937. Built to the new Vickers-Wallis patented constructional method known as the Geodetic System, the Wellesley was issued to seven squadrons of Bomber Command and four squadrons of Middle East Command during the period 1937-39. By the outbreak of war, the Bomber Command units had been re-equipped with other types.

Aircraft and personnel of Nos. 105 and 226 Battle Squadrons at Harwell (Berks) in November 1937. One of the main Expansion Scheme types, the Battle became the standard equipment of an entire Group—No. 2—during the period 1937-39. Although it was obsolescent by the outbreak of war, it remained in first-line service until late 1940. [*Aeroplane*

In addition to the several flying training schools in the U.K., there was in pre-war days one such unit outside Great Britain—No. 4 F.T.S. based at Abu Sueir in the Suez Canal Zone. Picture shows the school's Hawker Audaxes lined up ready for pupils to give a flying display on passing-out day, February 16, 1938. Note the engine decking louvres which were introduced in a number of Kestrel-engined Hart variants to provide additional breathing in the tropics.

Periodical inspection of the Rolls-Royce Kestrel engines of a Singapore III of No. 203 Squadron, Basrah, Iraq, in May 1938.

An Audax and a Fury I of No. 3 F.T.S., South Cerney (Glos), during a gunnery
affiliation exercise.                                    [Aeroplane

A Hart Trainer flies overhead during the annual camp of the Oxford University
Air Squadron.                                          [Charles E. Brown

R.A.F. trainee electricians learn their trade with the aid of some tired and tattered Bulldog airframes.

H.M. King George VI being greeted by A.V.M. Gossage on arrival at Northolt during his tour of R.A.F. stations on May 9, 1938. In the back-ground is the Airspeed Envoy G-AEXX which was then used by the Royal Household and operated by the King's Flight. Its wings and tailplane were painted silver, the rest of the machine being finished in the red and blue livery of the Guards.                            [*Christopher Cole*

Avro Anson of No. 220 Squadron flying over some battleships. The Anson entered service in March 1936 with No. 48 Squadron at Manston (Kent). In so doing it became the first monoplane to enter squadron service under the R.A.F. Expansion Scheme and also the first operational R.A.F. machine to employ a retractable undercarriage.

[*Charles E. Brown*

R.A.F. Expansion Scheme—factory scenes. Armstrong Whitworth Whitleys in production at Coventry.           [*Aeroplane*

Bristol Blenheims in production at Bristol.

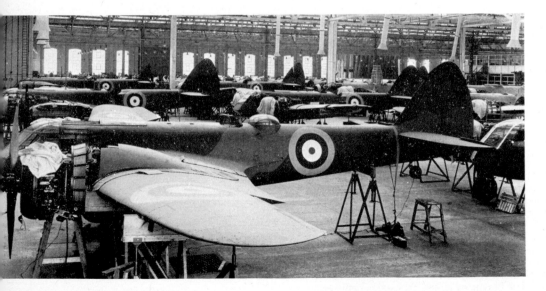

Vickers Wellingtons in production at Weybridge.

Hawker Hurricanes in production at Kingston-on-Thames.　　　[*Aeroplane*

Supermarine Spitfires in production at Woolston.

[*Aeroplane*

Miles Masters (*above*) and Magisters (*below*) awaiting delivery at Woodley.

Early production Hurricane I in flight.

[*Cyril Peckham*

Barrage balloons in the former airship hangar at Cardington (Beds) on the occasion of the Empire Air Day preview, May 1938.  In the foreground is a Wapiti.

The pre-war series of R.A.F. Displays at Hendon ended in 1937;  but in May 1938, and again in May 1939, there was an Empire Air Day at which selected R.A.F. stations throughout the country were open to the public in a similar manner to the Battle of Britain 'at homes' of today.  Below is a scene at Biggin Hill, featuring a Harrow and a Swordfish at the 1938 Empire Air Day display.  [*Aeroplane*

Blenheims of No. 44 Squadron, Waddington (Lincs), in May 1938.   Note the external bomb racks.  At the time of its introduction into service, the Blenheim was considered to be the fastest medium bomber in the world;  its top speed was 260 m.p.h.

Vickers Vildebeeste torpedo bombers at Alor Star, Malaya, in 1938.  They were on detachment from Seletar, Singapore, where two squadrons of these air-craft—Nos. 36 and 100—were maintained during the 1930s for the defence of the naval base and co-operation with the Fleet.

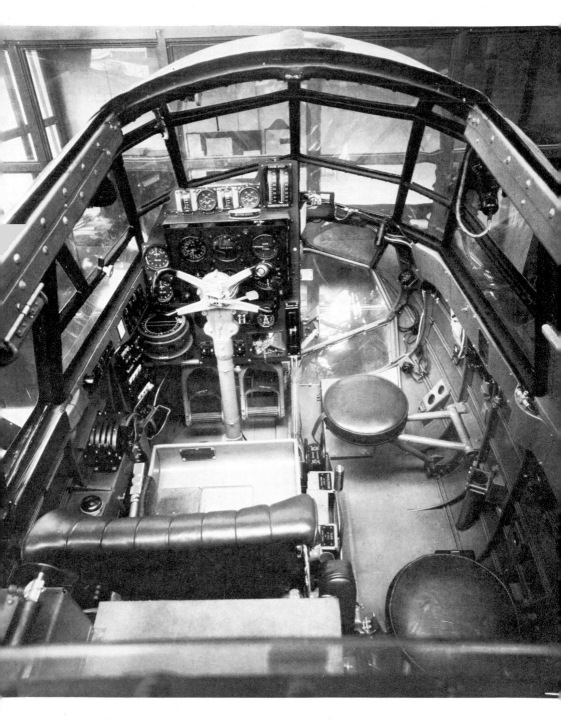

Cockpit of a Blenheim I.

Wapiti IIa's of No. 60 Squadron at Miramshah Fort in Northern Waziristan, during operations against recalcitrant tribesmen in June 1938. A few Wapitis soldiered on in India until after the outbreak of World War II.

'Week-end pilot' of No. 600 (City of London) Fighter Squadron, Auxiliary Air Force, receiving instruction in aerial gunnery at the firing butts at Hendon in 1938. The aircraft is a Demon.

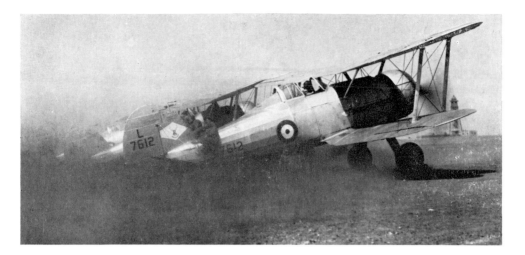

Gladiators of No. 33 Squadron make a dusty start-up at their base at Ismailia, Egypt, in August 1938.

V.I.P. visitor. Lord Trenchard seen after a flight in a D.H.86B of No. 24 Squadron in the late 1930s. *[Aeroplane*

*Above:* The C.O. of 'Treble-One' Squadron climbs into his Hurricane at Northolt, as mechanics start the engine ready for a night sortie during the Air Exercises in August 1938. *[Aeroplane*

*Left hand page:* Wellesley of Middle East Command being refuelled during an air exercise in 1938.

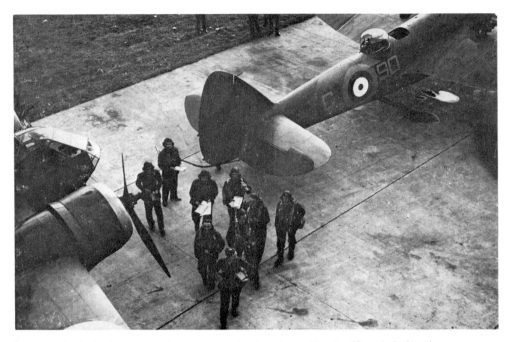

Blenheim 1 aircraft and crew of No. 90 Squadron, Bicester (Oxon) during the Air Defence Exercises of August 1938.                    [*Aeroplane*

Airmen prepare to load dummy torpedoes on to Vildebeeste IVs of No. 42 Squadron at Thorney Island (Hants) during an air exercise in 1938.

In 1938 the second prototype Westland Lysander army co-operation aircraft was shipped to India for tropical and field trials with No. 5 Squadron. Picture shows it in August 1938 on temporary gun butts erected by No. 31 Squadron at Drigh Road, Karachi.

Vic of three Airspeed Oxford advanced trainers of No. 3 Flying Training School, South Cerney (Glos) in August 1938.                                    [*Aeroplane*

When the Munich crisis came in September 1938, all first-line aircraft hitherto silver doped were hastily camouflaged and their squadron markings removed, sometimes to be replaced immediately by code letters.   At the same time their national markings were rendered less conspicuous and very often their serial numbers were obliterated too, to varying degrees—as was the case with these Gauntlets of No. 151 Squadron based at North Weald (*above*) and (*below*) Furies of No. 43 Squadron, Tangmere.

[*Lower photo: Flight International*

Short Sunderland L2160 of No. 230 Squadron being christened *Selangor* at Port Swettenham, Malaya, in October 1938. No. 230 Squadron was the first to be completely re-equipped with Sunderlands and L2160 was one of three 'originals' that were paid for by a gift of £300,000 from the Sultans of the Federated Malay States and ceremonially named in Malaya's honour.

Two airmen, watched by examiners, take a trade test on an Audax instructional airframe.

*[Aeroplane*

On November 5, 1938, three specially-modified Wellesleys of the R.A.F. Long-range Development Flight took off from Ismailia, Egypt, to fly non-stop to Darwin, Australia.  One machine (shown in the photograph) landed at Kupang before crossing the Timor Sea, but the other two reached Darwin on November 7 having flown 7,162 miles in just over 48 hours—and having broken the world's distance record.

This study of six Ansons of No. 217 Squadron flying over Chichester, early in 1939, provides a good example of the efficacy of camouflage. One machine is finished in 'sea' camouflage and the others in the standard 'land' scheme.

[W. A. Barton

No. 19 Squadron's Spitfires in the air early in 1939. Note that some of the machines lack wing roundels.

[Aeroplane

Largest educational establishment in the R.A.F. is No. 1 School of Technical Training at Halton, near Wendover (Bucks)—among lovely woods and overlooking the fertile green plains below. Established as a training camp during the 1914-18 War, Halton afterwards became the centre for the training of boy apprentices who were entering the R.A.F in the non-flying, non-commissioned ranks (although a few of them were regularly selected for commissions, and some became pilots). By the spring of 1938 some 5,000 boys between 15 and 17 years of age were studying at Halton and it was such boys who in pre-war days, as now, formed the backbone of the Regular R.A.F. technical branch. Picture shows apprentices marching past ground instructional airframes— 'pensioned-off' Blenheim Is and Battles—at Halton before the war. Halton was then the instructional centre for all technical work except wireless and electrical, which were taught in the Electrical and Wireless School at Cranwell.                                                                 [Aeroplane

'Flying suitcases': Handley Page Hampdens of No. 144 Squadron, Hemswell (Lincs) circa May 1939. The Hampden first entered squadron service in September 1938 and became standard equipment of No. 5 Group.

A 1939 Empire Air Day scene at Odiham (Hants) featuring a Miles Mentor, a Blenheim IV of No. 53 Squadron, an Anson and a Lysander.

[*Aeroplane*

Wellingtons of No. 149 Squadron which led a large formation of French and British aircraft over Paris on July 14, 1939, as part of the city's Bastille Day celebrations. At the bottom of the photograph *les Invalides* is clearly seen. [*Charles E. Brown*

Lysanders of No. 208 Squadron, Middle East Command
flying over the pyramids in 1939.  First unit to receive
Lysanders, or 'Lizzies' as they were popularly known, was
No. 16 Squadron at Old Sarum  (Wilts)  in June 1938.

[*Charles E. Brown*

A Hurricane of No. 56 Squadron being started by a trolley-acc. during the Air
Exercises in August 1939. [*Flight International*

Tiger-engined Whitleys of Nos. 51 and 58 Squadrons at Driffield (Yorks)
during the Air Exercises in August 1939. The Whitley was the standard
equipment of No. 4 Group, and when war was declared on September 3, 1939,
eight machines of Nos. 51 and 58 Squadrons were already standing by loaded
with the propaganda leaflets which the Government had decreed should be
dropped on Germany rather than bombs.

Pastoral. Hurricanes of No. 87 Squadron take off over
Blenheim IFs of No. 29 Squadron at Debden (Essex)
during the Air Exercises, August 1939, when war was
just a few weeks away.                    [*Aeroplane*